Mathematics Level **F**

PEOPLES
Common Core

Seeds for Success!

From the publisher of *Measuring Up*

peopleseducation.com

Peoples Education
Your partner in student success

Executive Vice President, Chief Creative Officer: Diane Miller

Editorial Development: Publisher's Partnership

Managing Editor: Kerri Gero

Editorial Assistant: Amy Priddy Wierzbicki

Copy Editor: Katy Leclercq

Vice President of Marketing: Victoria Ameer Kiely

Senior Marketing Manager: Christine Grasso

Marketing Manager: Victoria Leo

Production Director: Jason Grasso

Production Manager: Jennifer Bridges Brewer

Assistant Production Managers: Steven Genzano, Jennifer Tully

Director of Permissions: Kristine Liebman

Cover Design: Joe Guerrero, Todd Kochakji

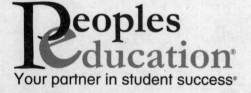

Peoples Education®
Your partner in student success®

Copyright © 2011
Peoples Education, Inc.
299 Market Street
Saddle Brook, New Jersey 07663

ISBN 978-1-61734-669-9

Printed in the United States of America.

Manufactured in Massachusetts in January 2013 by Bradford & Bigelow.

10   9   8   7   6

Table of Contents

Your teacher may choose to assign the pretest to diagnose your CCSS proficiency and direct you to help in this worktext.

CHAPTER 1 Ratio & Proportional Relationships

CHAPTER 2 The Number System

CHAPTER 3 Expressions & Equations

CHAPTER 4 Geometry

CHAPTER 5 Statistics & Probability

Your teacher may choose to assign the posttest for this program to check your learning.

Practice Path
Check out our Common Core web-based programs for access to thousands of additional practice items.

Grade 6 Common Core State Standards Overview

Ratios and Proportional Relationships
• Understand ratio concepts and use ratio reasoning to solve problems.

The Number System
• Apply and extend previous understandings of multiplication and division to divide fractions by fractions.

• Compute fluently with multi-digit numbers and find common factors and multiples.

• Apply and extend previous understandings of numbers to the system of rational numbers.

Expressions and Equations
• Apply and extend previous understandings of arithmetic to algebraic expressions.

• Reason about and solve one-variable equations and inequalities.

• Represent and analyze quantitative relationships between dependent and independent variables.

Geometry
• Solve real-world and mathematical problems involving area, surface area, and volume.

Statistics and Probability
• Develop understanding of statistical variability.

• Summarize and describe distributions.

Mathematical Practices
1. Make sense of problems and persevere in solving them.
2. Reason abstractly and quantitatively.
3. Construct viable arguments and critique the reasoning of others.
4. Model with mathematics.
5. Use appropriate tools strategically.
6. Attend to precision.
7. Look for and make use of structure.
8. Look for and express regularity in repeated reasoning.

Correlation to the Common Core State Standards

This worktext is customized to the Common Core State Standards for Mathematics. Most lessons focus on one content standard for in-depth review. Mathematical Practices are interwoven throughout each lesson to connect practices to content at point-of-use and promote depth of understanding.

Common Core State Standards	Lessons
Mathematical Practices	
1. Make sense of problems and persevere in solving them.	embedded throughout
2. Reason abstractly and quantitatively.	embedded throughout
3. Construct viable arguments and critique the reasoning of others.	embedded throughout
4. Model with mathematics.	embedded throughout
5. Use appropriate tools strategically.	embedded throughout
6. Attend to precision.	embedded throughout
7. Look for and make use of structure.	embedded throughout
8. Look for and express regularity in repeated reasoning.	embedded throughout
6.RP Ratios and Proportional Relationships	
Understand ratio concepts and use ratio reasoning to solve problems.	
1. Understand the concept of a ratio and use ratio language to describe a ratio relationship between two quantities. *For example, "The ratio of wings to beaks in the bird house at the zoo was 2:1, because for every 2 wings there was 1 beak." "For every vote candidate A received, candidate C received nearly three votes."*	1
2. Understand the concept of a unit rate $\frac{a}{b}$ associated with a ratio a:b with b ≠ 0, and use rate language in the context of a ratio relationship. *For example, "This recipe has a ratio of 3 cups of flour to 4 cups of sugar, so there is $\frac{3}{4}$ cup of flour for each cup of sugar." "We paid $75 for 15 hamburgers, which is a rate of $5 per hamburger."*1	2, 3
3. Use ratio and rate reasoning to solve real-world and mathematical problems, e.g., by reasoning about tables of equivalent ratios, tape diagrams, double number line diagrams, or equations.	4, 5, 6, 7, 8
a. Make tables of equivalent ratios relating quantities with whole-number measurements, find missing values in the tables, and plot the pairs of values on the coordinate plane. Use tables to compare ratios.	4, 5

vi

Common Core State Standards	Lessons
b. Solve unit rate problems including those involving unit pricing and constant speed. For example, if it took 7 hours to mow 4 lawns, then at that rate, how many lawns could be mowed in 35 hours? At what rate were lawns being mowed?	6
c. Find a percent of a quantity as a rate per 100 (e.g., 30% of a quantity means $\frac{30}{100}$ times the quantity); solve problems involving finding the whole, given a part and the percent.	7
d. Use ratio reasoning to convert measurement units; manipulate and transform units appropriately when multiplying or dividing quantities.	8
6.NS The Number System	
Apply and extend previous understandings of multiplication and division to divide fractions by fractions.	
1. Interpret and compute quotients of fractions, and solve word problems involving division of fractions by fractions, e.g., by using visual fraction models and equations to represent the problem. *For example, create a story context for (2/3) ÷ (3/4) and use a visual fraction model to show the quotient; use the relationship between multiplication and division to explain that (2/3) ÷ (3/4) = 8/9 because 3/4 of 8/9 is 2/3. (In general, (a/b) ÷ (c/d) = ad/bc.) How much chocolate will each person get if 3 people share 1/2 lb of chocolate equally? How many 3/4-cup servings are in 2/3 of a cup of yogurt? How wide is a rectangular strip of land with length 3/4 mi and area 1/2 square mi? Compute fluently with multi-digit numbers and find common factors and multiples.*	9, 10
Compute fluently with multi-digit numbers and find common factors and multiples.	
2. Fluently divide multi-digit numbers using the standard algorithm.	11
3. Fluently add, subtract, multiply, and divide multi-digit decimals using the standard algorithm for each operation.	12, 13
4. Find the greatest common factor of two whole numbers less than or equal to 100 and the least common multiple of two whole numbers less than or equal to 12. Use the distributive property to express a sum of two whole numbers 1–100 with a common factor as a multiple of a sum of two whole numbers with no common factor. *For example, express 36 + 8 as 4 (9 + 2). Apply and extend previous understandings of numbers to the system of rational numbers.*	14, 15
Apply and extend previous understandings of numbers to the system of rational numbers.	
5. Understand that positive and negative numbers are used together to describe quantities having opposite directions or values (e.g., temperature above/below zero, elevation above/below sea level, credits/debits, positive/negative electric charge); use positive and negative numbers to represent quantities in real-world contexts, explaining the meaning of 0 in each situation.	16
6. Understand a rational number as a point on the number line. Extend number line diagrams and coordinate axes familiar from previous grades to represent points on the line and in the plane with negative number coordinates.	17, 18, 19
a. Recognize opposite signs of numbers as indicating locations on opposite sides of 0 on the number line; recognize that the opposite of the opposite of a number is the number itself, e.g., −(−3) = 3, and that 0 is its own opposite.	17
b. Understand signs of numbers in ordered pairs as indicating locations in quadrants of the coordinate plane; recognize that when two ordered pairs differ only by signs, the locations of the points are related by reflections across one or both axes.	18
c. Find and position integers and other rational numbers on a horizontal or vertical number line diagram; find and position pairs of integers and other rational numbers on a coordinate plane.	19

Common Core State Standards	Lessons
7. Understand ordering and absolute value of rational numbers.	20, 21, 22, 23
a. Interpret statements of inequality as statements about the relative position of two numbers on a number line diagram. *For example, interpret –3 > –7 as a statement that –3 is located to the right of –7 on a number line oriented from left to right.*	20
b. Write, interpret, and explain statements of order for rational numbers in real-world contexts. *For example, write –3 °C > –7 °C to express the fact that –3 °C is warmer than –7 °C.*	21
c. Understand the absolute value of a rational number as its distance from 0 on the number line; interpret absolute value as magnitude for a positive or negative quantity in a real-world situation. *For example, for an account balance of –30 dollars, write $\lvert -30 \rvert = 30$ to describe the size of the debt in dollars.*	22
d. Distinguish comparisons of absolute value from statements about order. *For example, recognize that an account balance less than –30 dollars represents a debt greater than 30 dollars.*	23
8. Solve real-world and mathematical problems by graphing points in all four quadrants of the coordinate plane. Include use of coordinates and absolute value to find distances between points with the same first coordinate or the same second coordinate.	24
6.EE Expressions and Equations	
Apply and extend previous understandings of arithmetic to algebraic expressions.	
1. Write and evaluate numerical expressions involving whole-number exponents.	25
2. Write, read, and evaluate expressions in which letters stand for numbers.	26, 27, 28
a. Write expressions that record operations with numbers and with letters standing for numbers. *For example, express the calculation "Subtract y from 5" as $5 - y$.*	26
b. Identify parts of an expression using mathematical terms (sum, term, product, factor, quotient, coefficient); view one or more parts of an expression as a single entity. *For example, describe the expression 2 (8 + 7) as a product of two factors; view (8 + 7) as both a single entity and a sum of two terms.*	27
c. Evaluate expressions at specific values of their variables. Include expressions that arise from formulas used in real-world problems. Perform arithmetic operations, including those involving whole-number exponents, in the conventional order when there are no parentheses to specify a particular order (Order of Operations). *For example, use the formulas $V = s^3$ and $A = 6 s^2$ to find the volume and surface area of a cube with sides of length s = 1/2.*	28
3. Apply the properties of operations to generate equivalent expressions. *For example, apply the distributive property to the expression 3 (2 + x) to produce the equivalent expression 6 + 3x; apply the distributive property to the expression 24x + 18y to produce the equivalent expression 6 (4x + 3y); apply properties of operations to y + y + y to produce the equivalent expression 3y.*	29
4. Identify when two expressions are equivalent (i.e., when the two expressions name the same number regardless of which value is substituted into them). *For example, the expressions y + y + y and 3y are equivalent because they name the same number regardless of which number y stands for. Reason about and solve one-variable equations and inequalities.*	30
Reason about and solve one-variable equations and inequalities.	
5. Understand solving an equation or inequality as a process of answering a question: which values from a specified set, if any, make the equation or inequality true? Use substitution to determine whether a given number in a specified set makes an equation or inequality true.	31

Common Core State Standards	Lessons
6. Use variables to represent numbers and write expressions when solving a real-world or mathematical problem; understand that a variable can represent an unknown number, or, depending on the purpose at hand, any number in a specified set.	32
7. Solve real-world and mathematical problems by writing and solving equations of the form $x + p = q$ and $px = q$ for cases in which p, q and x are all nonnegative rational numbers.	33
8. Write an inequality of the form $x > c$ or $x < c$ to represent a constraint or condition in a real-world or mathematical problem. Recognize that inequalities of the form $x > c$ or $x < c$ have infinitely many solutions; represent solutions of such inequalities on number line diagrams.	34
Represent and analyze quantitative relationships between dependent and independent variables.	
9. Use variables to represent two quantities in a real-world problem that change in relationship to one another; write an equation to express one quantity, thought of as the dependent variable, in terms of the other quantity, thought of as the independent variable. Analyze the relationship between the dependent and independent variables using graphs and tables, and relate these to the equation. For example, in a problem involving motion at constant speed, list and graph ordered pairs of distances and times, and write the equation d = 65t to represent the relationship between distance and time.	35
6.G Geometry	
Solve real-world and mathematical problems involving area, surface area, and volume.	
1. Find the area of right triangles, other triangles, special quadrilaterals, and polygons by composing into rectangles or decomposing into triangles and other shapes; apply these techniques in the context of solving real-world and mathematical problems.	36, 37
2. Find the volume of a right rectangular prism with fractional edge lengths by packing it with unit cubes of the appropriate unit fraction edge lengths, and show that the volume is the same as would be found by multiplying the edge lengths of the prism. Apply the formulas $V = l\,w\,h$ and $V = b\,h$ to find volumes of right rectangular prisms with fractional edge lengths in the context of solving real-world and mathematical problems.	38
3. Draw polygons in the coordinate plane given coordinates for the vertices; use coordinates to find the length of a side joining points with the same first coordinate or the same second coordinate. Apply these techniques in the context of solving real-world and mathematical problems.	39
4. Represent three-dimensional figures using nets made up of rectangles and triangles, and use the nets to find the surface area of these figures. Apply these techniques in the context of solving real-world and mathematical problems.	40, 41
6.SP Statistics and Probability	
Develop understanding of statistical variability.	
1. Recognize a statistical question as one that anticipates variability in the data related to the question and accounts for it in the answers. *For example, "How old am I?" is not a statistical question, but "How old are the students in my school?" is a statistical question because one anticipates variability in students' ages.*	42
2. Understand that a set of data collected to answer a statistical question has a distribution which can be described by its center, spread, and overall shape.	43
3. Recognize that a measure of center for a numerical data set summarizes all of its values with a single number, while a measure of variation describes how its values vary with a single number.	43

Common Core State Standards	Lessons
Summarize and describe distributions.	
4. Display numerical data in plots on a number line, including dot plots, histograms, and box plots.	44, 45, 46
5. Summarize numerical data sets in relation to their context, such as by:	44, 45, 46, 47, 48
a. Reporting the number of observations.	47
b. Describing the nature of the attribute under investigation, including how it was measured and its units of measurement.	47
c. Giving quantitative measures of center (median and/or mean) and variability (interquartile range and/or mean absolute deviation), as well as describing any overall pattern and any striking deviations from the overall pattern with reference to the context in which the data were gathered.	44, 45, 46
d. Relating the choice of measures of center and variability to the shape of the data distribution and the context in which the data were gathered.	48

Common Core

To the Student:

It's never too soon to prepare for your future. The same goes for learning the new Common Core State Standards for your grade level. This new set of expectations will help you be prepared for college and your career, and to be successful in all your academic pursuits.

The lessons in this book are geared toward helping you master all the Common Core State Standards for mathematics in a structured way.

Peoples Common Core has 5 chapters, each one is focused on a different set of skills and modeled on the Common Core State Standards.

Each chapter includes:

• A brief review of skills and key vocabulary

• Suggested tools to help you learn

• Real world examples

• Step-by-step problem-solving instruction

• A variety of activities and questions that allow you to show your learning

• Multiple-choice, short-answer, and extended-response question practice

• A special Kick It Up project and activity to boost your learning to the next level

These lessons will help you build your mathematics skills and improve your high-level thinking. The lessons may seem challenging at first, but keep at it and you will be a success!

Have a great school year!

To Parents and Families:

Peoples Education has created this Common Core book to help your child master the new Common Core State Standards, and to get your child to think on a higher level. The Common Core State Standards are a clear set of K–12 grade-specific expectations. Developed by a consortium of states and coordinated by the National Governors Association and the Council of Chief State School Officers, these standards define what it means for students to be college- and career-ready in the 21st century. As your child moves through this book, encourage your child to consider, analyze, interpret, and evaluate instead of just recalling simple facts.

Each of the 5 chapters in this book is focused on a different set of skills, modeled on the Common Core State Standards.

Each chapter includes:

- A review of skills and key vocabulary
- Real world examples
- Step-by-step problem-solving instruction
- A variety of activities and questions that allow your child to show his or her skill comprehension
- Multiple-choice, short-answer, and extended-response question practice
- A special Kick It Up project and activity to boost your child's learning to the next level

For success in school and the real world, your child needs a solid mathematics foundation, and your involvement is crucial to that success. Here are some suggestions:

Show that mathematics is important, by including your child in activities that require mathematical thinking.

Help find appropriate Internet sites for mathematics. Note how mathematics is used when you are out with your family. Discuss how mathematics is used in financial and banking matters, in careers such as engineering, architecture, and medicine, in space exploration, and in other real-life situations.

Encourage your child to take time to review and check his or her homework. Just solving a problem is not enough. Ask your child whether the answer is reasonable and have him or her explain what led to that answer.

Get involved! Work with us this year to ensure your child's success. Mathematics skills are an essential part of college and career readiness and the real world.

Peoples Education
Your partner in student success

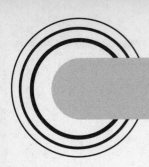

What's Inside

Lessons in this worktext provide instruction, activities, and review for each skill in the Common Core State Standards.

Real World Connections helps you understand the skill with examples and problems from real life. Toolbox lists supplies needed for the lesson and Key Words highlight the words you will need to know.

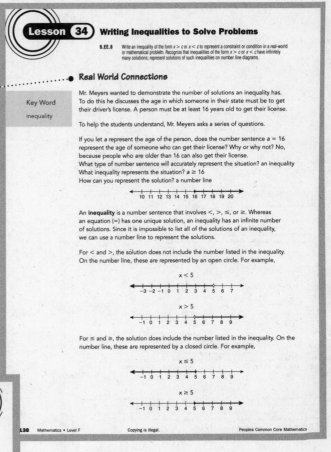

Lesson 34 Writing Inequalities to Solve Problems

6.EE.8 Write an inequality of the form $x > c$ or $x < c$ to represent a constraint or condition in a real-world or mathematical problem. Recognize that inequalities of the form $x > c$ or $x < c$ have infinitely many solutions; represent solutions of such inequalities on number line diagrams.

Real World Connections

Key Word
inequality

Mr. Meyers wanted to demonstrate the number of solutions an inequality has. To do this he discusses the age in which someone in their state must be to get their driver's license. A person must be at least 16 years old to get their license.

To help the students understand, Mr. Meyers asks a series of questions.

If you let a represent the age of the person, does the number sentence $a = 16$ represent the age of someone who can get their license? Why or why not? No, because people who are older than 16 can also get their license.
What type of number sentence will accurately represent the situation? an inequality
What inequality represents the situation? $a \geq 16$
How can you represent the solution? a number line

An **inequality** is a number sentence that involves $<$, $>$, $\leq$, or $\geq$. Whereas an equation $(=)$ has one unique solution, an inequality has an infinite number of solutions. Since it is impossible to list all of the solutions of an inequality, we can use a number line to represent the solutions.

For $<$ and $>$, the solution does not include the number listed in the inequality. On the number line, these are represented by an open circle. For example,

$x < 5$

$x > 5$

For $\leq$ and $\geq$, the solution does include the number listed in the inequality. On the number line, these are represented by a closed circle. For example,

$x \leq 5$

$x \geq 5$

138   Mathematics • Level F   Copying is illegal.   Peoples Common Core Mathematics

Writing Inequalities to Solve Problems **34 Lesson**

Take It Apart

Kirri has a savings account in which she wants to maintain a balance that is more than $150. Write a number sentence that represents the situation. Graph the solution.

Step 1 Define any variables. Identify key words in the problem.

Let b represent the balance of the savings account. The words "is more than" indicates that the number sentence will be an inequality with $>$.

Step 2 Write a number sentence that represents the situation.
$b > 150$

Step 3 Use a number line to graph the solution.

100 110 120 130 140 150 160 170 180 190 200

If necessary, solve the inequality showing your work. Graph the solution.

1. $n \leq -3$

–6 –5 –4 –3 –2 –1 0 1 2 3 4

2. $x + 1 \geq 4$

_____

–4 –3 –2 –1 0 1 2 3 4 5 6

Take It Apart helps you solve a problem step-by-step to build your skills.

Answer each question.

1. The amusement park ride has a sign that says all riders must be a minimum of 48 inches tall. Write a number sentence to represent this situation. Graph the solution.

43 44 45 46 47 48 49 50 51 52 53

2. The sign on the road indicates the speed limit is 55 miles per hour. Write a number sentence to represent this situation. Graph the solution.

50 51 52 53 54 55 56 57 58 59 60

3. The menu says that children under the age of 5 eat free. Write a number sentence to represent this situation. Graph the solution.

1 2 3 4 5 6 7 8 9 10 11

Put It Together asks you to apply the skill with different types of questions and activities.

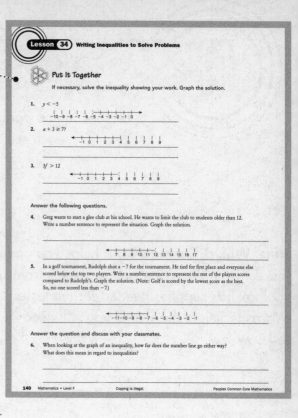

Put It Together

If necessary, solve the inequality showing your work. Graph the solution.

1. $y < -5$

2. $a + 3 \geq 7?$

3. $3f > 12$

Answer the following questions.

4. Greg wants to start a glee club at his school. He wants to limit the club to students older than 12. Write a number sentence to represent the situation. Graph the solution.

5. In a golf tournament, Rudolph shot a -7 for the tournament. He tied for first place and everyone else scored below the top two players. Write a number sentence to represent the rest of the players scores compared to Rudolph's. Graph the solution. (Note: Golf is scored by the lowest score as the best. So, no one scored less than -7.)

Answer the question and discuss with your classmates.

6. When looking at the graph of an inequality, how far does the number line go either way? What does this mean in regard to inequalities?

140   Mathematics • Level F   Copying is illegal.   Peoples Common Core Mathematics

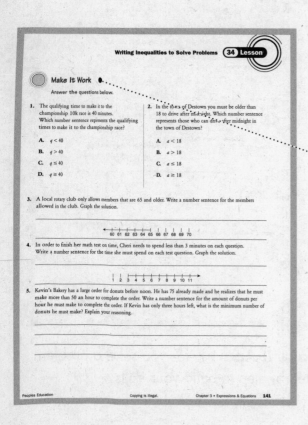

Writing Inequalities to Solve Problems **34** Lesson

Make It Work

Answer the questions below.

1. The qualifying time to make it to the championship 10k race is 40 minutes. Which number sentence represents the qualifying times to make it to the championship race?
   A. $q < 40$
   B. $q > 40$
   C. $q \leq 40$
   D. $q \geq 40$

2. In the town of Destown you must be older than 18 to drive after midnight. Which number sentence represents those who can drive after midnight in the town of Destown?
   A. $a < 18$
   B. $a > 18$
   C. $a \leq 18$
   D. $a \geq 18$

3. A local rotary club only allows members that are 65 and older. Write a number sentence for the members allowed in the club. Graph the solution.

4. In order to finish her math test on time, Cheri needs to spend less than 3 minutes on each question. Write a number sentence for the time she must spend on each test question. Graph the solution.

5. Kevin's Bakery has a large order for donuts before noon. He has 75 already made and he realizes that he must make more than 50 an hour to complete the order. Write a number sentence for the amount of donuts per hour he must make to complete the order. If Kevin has only three hours left, what is the minimum number of donuts he must make? Explain your reasoning.

Peoples Education   Copying is illegal.   Chapter 3 • Expressions & Equations   **141**

Make It Work assesses your learning on the lesson skill with a variety of formats, including multiple-choice, short-answer, and extended-response questions.

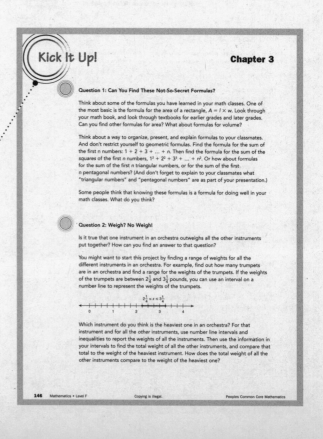

Kick It Up!   **Chapter 3**

Question 1: Can You Find These Not-So-Secret Formulas?

Think about some of the formulas you have learned in your math classes. One of the most basic is the formula for the area of a rectangle, $A = l \times w$. Look through your math book, and look through textbooks for earlier grades and later grades. Can you find other formulas for area? What about formulas for volume?

Think about a way to organize, present, and explain formulas to your classmates. And don't restrict yourself to geometric formulas. Find the formula for the sum of the first n numbers: $1 + 2 + 3 + \dots + n$. Then find the formula for the sum of the squares of the first n numbers, $1^2 + 2^2 + 3^2 + \dots + n^2$. Or how about formulas for the sum of the first n triangular numbers, or for the sum of the first n pentagonal numbers? (And don't forget to explain to your classmates what "triangular numbers" and "pentagonal numbers" are as part of your presentation.)

Some people think that knowing these formulas is a formula for doing well in your math classes. What do you think?

Question 2: Weigh? No Weigh!

Is it true that one instrument in an orchestra outweighs all the other instruments put together? How can you find an answer to that question?

You might want to start this project by finding a range of weights for all the different instruments in an orchestra. For example, find out how many trumpets are in an orchestra and find a range for the weights of the trumpets. If the weights of the trumpets are between $2\frac{1}{4}$ and $3\frac{1}{4}$ pounds, you can use an interval on a number line to represent the weights of the trumpets.

Which instrument do you think is the heaviest one in an orchestra? For that instrument and for all the other instruments, use number line intervals and inequalities to report the weights of all the instruments. Then use the information in your intervals to find the total weight of all the other instruments, and compare that total to the weight of the heaviest instrument. How does the total weight of all the other instruments compare to the weight of the heaviest one?

146   Mathematics • Level F   Copying is illegal.   Peoples Common Core Mathematics

Kick It Up end-of-chapter activities are fun projects to build your research, collaboration, problem-solving, technology, and writing skills.

6.RP.1 Understand the concept of a ratio and use ratio language to describe a ratio relationship between two quantities. *For example, "The ratio of wings to beaks in the bird house at the zoo was 2:1, because for every 2 wings there was 1 beak." "For every vote candidate A received, candidate C received nearly three votes."*

Real World Connections

Some engines require a special gas mixture. For example, the majority of 2-cycle engines, such as engines in many lawn mowers and weed eaters, use a fuel mixture that is part gas and part oil. This mixture contains a fixed number of each of its parts. To keep the engines running properly, the fuel must be mixed in the correct ratio.

The instruction manual for a riding lawn mower says to mix 80 ounces of gas with 2 ounces of oil. What is the ratio of gas to oil, written in simplest form, for this lawn mower?

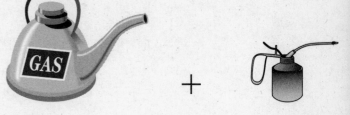

80 ounces gas   2 ounces oil

A **ratio** is a comparison of two numbers, often expressed as a fraction. A ratio can compare a part to a part, a part to a whole, or a whole to a part. A ratio can be written in any of the following forms.

$$\frac{a}{b} \qquad a{:}b \qquad a \text{ to } b$$

A ratio is in **simplest form** when its terms have no common factors other than 1. For example, the simplest form of 4:6 is 2:3 since 2 and 3 have no common factors other than 1. If the ratio is written in fraction form, reduce the fraction as much as possible to find the simplest form.

Two ratios are **equivalent ratios** if they have the same simplest form. For example, $\frac{16}{20}$ and $\frac{8}{10}$ are equivalent ratios since $\frac{16}{20} = \frac{4}{5}$ and $\frac{8}{10} = \frac{4}{5}$.

Take It Apart

To write and simplify ratios, follow some simple steps.

Step 1 Read the problem carefully. Decide what quantities are being compared. Write the comparison using words.

> gas to oil

Step 2 Check to see if the units on the quantities are the same.

80 ounces **gas**   2 ounces **oil**

In this problem, the quantities are both given in ounces.

Step 3 Paying careful attention to the order of the words, replace the words with numbers from the problem. There is no need to include units since they are the same.

> 80 to 2

Step 4 Write the ratio as a fraction.

> $\dfrac{80}{2}$

Step 5 Write the ratio in simplest form by reducing the fraction. In this case, divide the numerator and denominator by 2 to reduce the fraction.

> $\dfrac{80 \div 2}{2 \div 2} = \dfrac{40}{1}$

The ratio of gas to oil in the mixture is $\dfrac{40}{1}$.

Use the strategy above to write a fraction, in simplest form, for each situation.

1. A recipe calls for 3 cups of flour and 1 cup of sugar. What is the ratio of flour to sugar?

   _____

2. In Mr. Jones' class, 22 students are right-handed and 4 are left-handed. What is the ratio of right-handed students to left-handed students?

   _____

3. Ten boys and 18 girls are going on the sixth-grade science trip. What is the ratio of girls to boys going on the trip?

   _____

4. There are 40 sixth-graders and 32 seventh-graders working on a highway cleanup project. What is the ratio of sixth-graders to the total number of students working on the project?

   _____

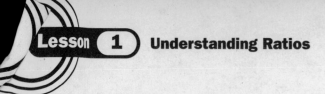

Lesson 1 **Understanding Ratios**

 Put It Together

Use what you now know about ratios to write a fraction, in simplest form, to represent each situation.

1. There are 21 roses and 18 tulips in Sara's garden. What is the ratio of roses to tulips in her garden?

_____

2. Marco found a box of books in his attic that contained 14 mysteries, 8 biographies, and 4 comics. What is the ratio of comics to mysteries in the box?

_____

3. There are 28 windows in Maria's house. She has washed 20 of the windows so far. What is the ratio of the number of windows she has washed to the number of windows she has not washed?

_____

4. Mrs. Clements is giving a math test with 40 multiple choice questions and 25 fill in the blanks. What is the ratio of the number of multiple choice questions on the test to the total number of questions on the test?

_____

Answer the questions. Share your ideas with a classmate.

5. There are 120 eighth-graders at a certain middle school. Ninety-six of them have already taken Beginning Algebra. What is the ratio of eighth-graders who have already taken Beginning Algebra to those who have not yet taken Beginning Algebra?

_____

_____

6. There are 12 tigers, 18 alligators, and 27 monkeys at the local zoo. Is the ratio of tigers to alligators equivalent to the ratio of alligators to monkeys? Why or why not?

_____

_____

_____

     Peoples Common Core Mathematics

Make It Work

Answer the questions below.

1. David has 54 marbles, 24 of which are black, 18 are red, and 12 are blue. Which fraction represents the ratio of black marbles to blue marbles?

    A. $\frac{2}{9}$ **B.** $\frac{1}{2}$

    C. $\frac{4}{3}$ **D.** $\frac{2}{1}$

2. What is the quotient of $\frac{8}{18} \div 2$?

    A. $\frac{2}{9}$ **B.** 8:18

    C. 4:9 **D.** $\frac{16}{36}$

3. Write three ratios, in fraction form, that are equivalent to the ratio $\frac{4}{5}$.

    _____

4. Mike's mom made two bags of mixed nuts. She put 14 ounces of peanuts and 8 ounces of almonds in the first bag. In the second bag, she put 12 ounces of almonds and 20 ounces of peanuts. She told Mike that the ratio of peanuts to almonds in both bags was the same. Was she correct? Why or why not?

    _____

    _____

5. Michelle's Craft Shoppe sells a package of beads that has a ratio of 30 red beads to 5 green beads. If 12 red beads are added to the package, how many green beads must be added in order for the ratio of bead colors to stay the same? Explain how you found your answer.

    _____

    _____

    _____

    _____

    _____

Lesson 2 — Understanding Unit Rates

6.RP.2 Understand the concept of a unit rate $\frac{a}{b}$ associated with a ratio $a{:}b$ with $b \neq 0$, and use rate language in the context of a ratio relationship. *For example, "This recipe has a ratio of 3 cups of flour to 4 cups of sugar, so there is $\frac{3}{4}$ cup of flour for each cup of sugar." "We paid $75 for 15 hamburgers, which is a rate of $5 per hamburger."*

Real World Connections

Key Words

rate

unit rate

A box of multi-grain crackers contains 8 servings and has a total of 600 calories. How many calories are in one serving?

A special type of ratio that compares two different kinds of quantities, such as calories and servings, is called a **rate**.

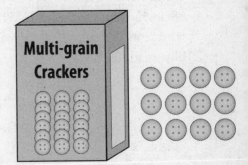

A **unit rate** is a rate that has a denominator of 1 and often contains the word *per*. Speed is a rate that is usually expressed as a unit rate. For example, 55 miles per hour can also be read as 55 miles per one hour.

Since a unit rate has a denominator of 1, to find the unit rate simply divide the numerator and the denominator by the denominator. For example, if Jose earns $54 for working 12 hours, then his unit rate is $\frac{\$54}{12 \text{ hours}} = \frac{\$54 \div 12}{12 \div 12 \text{ hours}} = \frac{\$4.50}{1 \text{ hour}}$ or $4.50 per hour.

There are many more examples of unit rates in the real world. Here are a few: gas mileage (miles per gallon), salaries (earnings per month), typing speed (words per minute), and pulse (heartbeats per minute).

Peoples Common Core Mathematics

Take It Apart

To find a unit rate, follow some simple steps.

Step 1 Use the word "per" to write the rate in words.

600 calories per 8 servings

Step 2 Write the rate as a fraction. The first term is always the numerator and the second term (the term after the word per) is always the denominator. Include the units since they are not the same unit for each term in the rate.

$$\frac{600 \text{ calories}}{8 \text{ servings}}$$

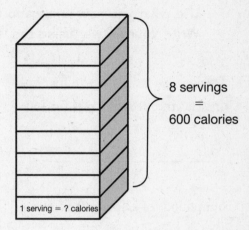

8 servings
=
600 calories

1 serving = ? calories

Step 3 Find the unit rate by dividing both the numerator and the denominator by the number in the denominator. The result will always be a denominator of 1.

$$\frac{600 \text{ calories}}{8 \text{ servings}} = \frac{600 \div 8 \text{ calories}}{8 \div 8 \text{ servings}} = \frac{75 \text{ calories}}{1 \text{ serving}}$$

Step 4 Write the unit rate back in words to answer the question.

75 calories per serving

There are 75 calories in one serving of the crackers.

Use the strategy above to find the unit rate for each situation. Write your answer using the word _per_.

1. Peter drove 208 miles in 4 hours.

   _____

2. There are 225 students on 5 buses. Each bus has the same number of students.

   _____

3. Shawn can type 154 words in 7 minutes.

   _____

4. An attorney charges $900 for 4 hours of work.

   _____

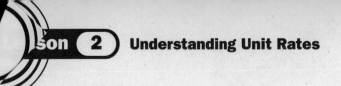
 Put It Together

Use what you now know about rates to find the unit rate for each situation. Write your answer using the word *per*.

1. Mrs. Hawthorne sells 8 pies for $60.

_____

2. A taxi traveled 336 miles and used 12 gallons of gas.

_____

3. Four pounds of grapes cost $5.60.

_____

4. Karen drove 279 miles in 4.5 hours.

_____

Use a unit rate to answer each question. Show your work.

5. Mary Beth traveled 240 miles in 4.8 hours and then stopped for a break. Then she traveled 255 miles in 4.2 hours. Not counting the break, what was Mary Beth's average speed for the whole trip?

_____

_____

_____

6. Darren is trying to improve his typing speed. On his first practice assignment, he typed 198 words in 6 minutes. On his second assignment, he typed 248 words in 8 minutes. Did his speed improve? Tell how you know.

_____

_____

_____

Make It Work

Answer the questions below.

1. A chemist makes a mixture using 6 cups of powder and 0.5 gallon of liquid. What is the unit rate of powder to liquid?

    A. 3 cups per gallon

    B. 6 cups per gallon

    C. 12 cups per gallon

    D. 24 cups per gallon

2. An airline manager found that during a 24-hour period, 1,440 passengers passed through one terminal. What was the unit rate of passenger flow?

    A. 60 passengers per minute

    B. 60 passengers per hour

    C. 120 passengers per minute

    D. 120 passengers per hour

3. A bunch of seven bananas weighs 3.5 pounds. The cost of the bunch is $3.08. What is the unit price per pound of the bananas?

_____

4. You burn about 300 calories by walking for one hour. How many calories do you burn per minute?

_____

5. If a car travels 23 miles in 20 minutes, what is the car's speed in miles per hour? Explain how you found your answer.

_____

_____

_____

_____

Lesson 3 Identifying Relationships Between Ratios

6.RP.2 Understand the concept of a unit rate $\frac{a}{b}$ associated with a ratio $a{:}b$ with $b \neq 0$, and use rate language in the context of a ratio relationship. *For example, "This recipe has a ratio of 3 cups of flour to 4 cups of sugar, so there is $\frac{3}{4}$ cup of flour for each cup of sugar." "We paid $75 for 15 hamburgers, which is a rate of $5 per hamburger."*

Real World Connections

Key Word

unit price

Fazeel needs to buy several pairs of socks. He finds one brand that has 4 pairs in a pack that sells for $6.96 and another brand that has 6 pairs in a pack that sells for $10.92. Which pack is the better buy?

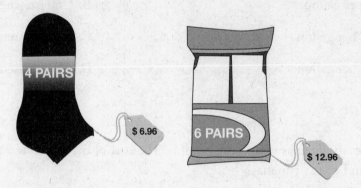

Recall that a unit rate is a rate that has a denominator of 1. Unit rates can be used to make comparisons and identify relationships between rates.

A unit rate can also be used to compare prices. When a unit rate involves a price, it is commonly called a **unit price**. If you write the rate with a denominator of 1, you are finding the price for exactly one item. For example, if you pay $1.56 for 12 pencils, the unit rate (or unit price) is $\frac{\$1.56}{12} = \frac{\$0.13}{1}$. This means the price of one pencil is 13 cents.

To identify the relationship between two rates, you can find the unit rate for each and compare. Identifying the better rate depends on the situation. For example, for gas mileage the better rate is the higher rate, but for price the better rate is the lower rate.

Take It Apart

To compare two rates, follow some simple steps.

Step 1 Write each of the rates as a fraction. Be sure to write the terms in the same order for each rate. Always include units so your final answer will make sense to you.

Black socks: $\dfrac{\$6.96}{4 \text{ pairs}}$ White socks: $\dfrac{\$12.96}{6 \text{ pairs}}$

Step 2 Find the unit rate for each by dividing.

Black socks: $\dfrac{\$6.96 \div 4}{4 \div 4 \text{ pairs}} = \dfrac{\$1.74}{1 \text{ pair}}$

White socks: $\dfrac{\$12.96 \div 6}{6 \div 6 \text{ pairs}} = \dfrac{\$2.16}{1 \text{ pair}}$

Step 3 Read the problem to see which rate is better based on the situation.

The better buy is the brand with the <u>lower</u> unit price. The black socks are the better buy.

Write the unit price for each item on the line. Then compare the unit prices and circle the better buy.

1. Strawberries: $1.50 for 1 basket or $5.00 for 4 baskets   _____

2. Eggs: $4.60 for 5 dozen or $2.94 for 3 dozen   _____

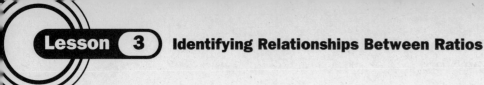

 ## Put It Together

Write each unit rate on the line. Then compare the rates. Circle the better rate. Keep in mind that the meaning of *better* depends on the situation.

1. Packs of notebooks:

   4-pack for $5.00 _____

   6-pack for $8.00 _____

2. Typing speeds, assuming no errors:

   Typist 1: 232 words in 8 minutes

   _____

   Typist 2: 217 words in 7 minutes

   _____

Answer each question.

3. When comparing salaries, which unit rate is better: $3,250/month or $4,000/month? Explain your answer.

   _____

   _____

4. Alexis has narrowed down her college choices to the three colleges shown in the table below. She plans to take the maximum number of classes allowed each semester. If she makes her decision based only on the best tuition rate per class, which college should she choose? Justify your answer using specific values.

	College A	College B	College C
Tuition per Semester	$2,224	$2,800	$3,270
Number of Classes Allowed per Semester	4	5	6

   _____

   _____

   _____

Make It Work

Answer the questions below.

1. Which jar of peanut butter is the best buy?

   A. 12 oz - $2.16

   B. 18 oz - $3.33

   C. 28 oz - $4.76

   D. 40 oz - $7.20

2. Which car has the best gas mileage rate?

   A. Car A travels 177 miles and uses 6 gallons

   B. Car B travels 208 miles and uses 6.5 gallons

   C. Car C travels 196 miles and uses 7 gallons

   D. Car D travels 170 miles and uses 5 gallons

3. Give three examples of rates for which a higher unit rate is the better rate.

   _____

4. Juanita is trying to decide which exercise machine she wants to use. The fitness trainer says that Juanita can burn about 165 calories by walking on a treadmill for 30 minutes or 150 calories by using the elliptical trainer for 25 minutes. If Juanita wants to use the machine with the better rate, which machine should she use? Justify your answer.

   _____

   _____

5. The table shows the number of hours worked and the total amount that each of four people earned one weekend. Whose pay rate was the best and whose pay rate was the worst? Explain your answer.

Name	Total	Number of Hours
Gary	$37.00	4
Tara	$54.90	6
Lamar	$27.60	3
Darius	$46.50	5

   _____

   _____

   _____

Lesson 4 — Making Tables of Equivalent Ratios

6.RP.3.a Make tables of equivalent ratios relating quantities with whole-number measurements, find missing values in the tables, and plot the pairs of values on the coordinate plane. Use tables to compare ratios.

Real World Connections

The table below is a table of ratios relating the amount of money a 9th-grader charges for tutoring to the number of hours he tutors. Use the table to determine how much this tutor charges for 5 hours of tutoring.

Total Cost $\overline{\text{Number of Hours}}$	$\frac{30}{2}$	$\frac{45}{3}$	$\frac{60}{4}$	$\frac{\square}{5}$

In an earlier lesson you learned that two ratios are equivalent if they have the same simplest form. In this lesson, you will use a different definition to determine whether two ratios are equivalent. Remember that a ratio can be written as a fraction.

A **cross product** is the product of the numerator of one fraction and the denominator of the other. The relationship below has two cross products, $a \times d$ and $c \times b$.

$$\frac{a}{b} \diagup\!\!\!\!\!\diagdown = \frac{c}{d}$$

Two ratios are **equivalent ratios** if the two cross products are equal.

For example, in the relationship $\frac{6}{12} = \frac{10}{20}$, the cross products are $6 \times 20 = 120$ and $10 \times 12 = 120$. Since the cross products are equal, the ratios $\frac{6}{12}$ and $\frac{10}{20}$ are equivalent ratios.

Take It Apart

To find an equivalent ratio, follow some simple steps.

Step 1   Examine the ratios in the table. Determine whether the ratios are equivalent using cross products.

Total Cost Number of Hours	$\frac{30}{2}$	$\frac{45}{3}$	$\frac{60}{4}$	$\frac{\square}{5}$

$$\frac{30}{2} \stackrel{?}{=} \frac{45}{3} \qquad \frac{30}{2} \stackrel{?}{=} \frac{60}{4} \qquad \frac{45}{3} \stackrel{?}{=} \frac{60}{4}$$

$$30 \times 3 \stackrel{?}{=} 45 \times 2 \quad 30 \times 4 \stackrel{?}{=} 60 \times 2 \quad 45 \times 4 \stackrel{?}{=} 60 \times 3$$

$$90 = 90 \qquad\qquad 120 = 120 \qquad\qquad 180 = 180$$

Yes, the ratios are all equivalent.

Step 2   Use any of the ratios to find the missing number. $\frac{30}{2} = \frac{?}{5}$

Write the cross products. $\qquad\qquad\qquad 30 \times 5 = 2 \times ?$

Find the missing number using division. $150 \div 2 = 75$

The missing equivalent ratio is $\frac{75}{5}$.

Step 3   Use the ratio to answer the question.

The tutor will charge $75 for 5 hours of tutoring.

Use the strategy above to fill in the missing ratios in each table.

1.

Brantley's Gas Mileage in $\frac{\text{miles}}{\text{gallons}}$			
Car	$\frac{56}{2}$	$\frac{84}{3}$	$\frac{112}{4}$	$\frac{\square}{5}$
Truck	$\frac{32}{2}$	$\frac{48}{3}$	$\frac{\square}{4}$	$\frac{80}{5}$

2.

Typing Speeds in $\frac{\text{words}}{\text{minutes}}$			
Typist 1	$\frac{\square}{10}$	$\frac{525}{15}$	$\frac{875}{25}$	$\frac{2,100}{60}$
Typist 2	$\frac{420}{10}$	$\frac{630}{15}$	$\frac{\square}{25}$	$\frac{2,520}{60}$

Put It Together

Use what you now know about equivalent ratios to fill in the missing values in each table.

1.

Ratios equivalent to the fraction $\frac{1}{2}$					
$\frac{2}{4}$	$\frac{5}{10}$	$\frac{\square}{16}$	$\frac{25}{50}$	$\frac{33}{66}$	$\frac{42}{\square}$

2.

Distance raveled at a constant speed in $\frac{miles}{hours}$				
$\frac{104}{2}$	$\frac{\square}{3}$	$\frac{234}{4.5}$	$\frac{364}{\square}$	$\frac{416}{8}$

3.

Cost for a plumber to work on a leak in $\frac{dollars}{hours}$			
Plumber 1	$\frac{55}{1}$	$\frac{110}{2}$	$\frac{\square}{5}$
Plumber 2	$\frac{\square}{16}$	$\frac{95}{2}$	$\frac{285}{6}$

4.

Measurement conversions			
Length $\left(\frac{inches}{feet}\right)$	$\frac{12}{1}$	$\frac{36}{3}$	$\frac{60}{\square}$
Time $\left(\frac{weeks}{days}\right)$	$\frac{2}{14}$	$\frac{5}{35}$	$\frac{\square}{84}$

Each row in the table contains equivalent ratios. Fill in the missing values. Then use the table to answer questions 5 and 6.

Attorney Costs $\left(\frac{dollars}{hours}\right)$				
Attorney A	$\frac{225}{1}$	$\frac{450}{2}$	$\frac{1,125}{5}$	$\frac{\square}{8}$
Attorney B	$\frac{\square}{1}$	$\frac{350}{2}$	$\frac{875}{5}$	$\frac{1,400}{8}$

5. How much would Attorney A charge for 8 hours of work? _____

6. If Attorney B increases his hourly rate by $15, how much would he charge for 4 hours of work? Explain how you found your answer.

_____

_____

_____

Make It Work

Answer the questions below.

1. Which ratio would not belong in the table of equivalent ratios below?

A	B	$\frac{10}{35}$	C	D

A. $\frac{2}{7}$

B. $\frac{8}{28}$

C. $\frac{16}{56}$

D. $\frac{20}{75}$

2. According to the table of equivalent ratios, how many inches are in 15 yards?

Length Conversions in $\frac{inches}{yards}$			
$\frac{72}{2}$	$\frac{180}{5}$	$\frac{432}{12}$	$\frac{???}{15}$

A. 468

B. 504

C. 540

D. 576

3. The table below contains ratios that are all equivalent. Fill in the missing values.

$\frac{3}{4}$	$\frac{6}{\Box}$	$\frac{\Box}{12}$	$\frac{15}{\Box}$	$\frac{\Box}{28}$	$\frac{30}{\Box}$	$\frac{\Box}{60}$

4. The table below shows the relationship between the number of hours of tutoring and the total cost for two different tutors. Each row consists of equivalent ratios $\left(\frac{dollars}{hours}\right)$. Use the table to answer the question.

Tutor 1	$\frac{45}{3}$	$\frac{60}{4}$	$\frac{90}{6}$
Tutor 2	$\frac{40}{2}$	$\frac{80}{4}$	$\frac{100}{5}$

If Margaret needs 2 hours of tutoring per week, how much more would she have to pay Tutor 2 than Tutor 1 per month? Assume there are 4 weeks in each month. Explain how you found your answer.

_____

_____

_____

_____

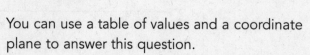

6.RP.3.a Make tables of equivalent ratios relating quantities with whole-number measurements, find missing values in the tables, and plot the pairs of values on the coordinate plane. Use tables to compare ratios.

Real World Connections

Key Words

- coordinate plane
- ordered pair
- *x*-coordinate
- *y*-coordinate

Mr. Martin begins filling his new swimming pool with water at noon. The rate at which the water is rising is 2 feet per hour. The user manual for the pool's filter instructs the user to turn the filter on when the depth of the water is 5 feet. At what time should the filter be turned on?

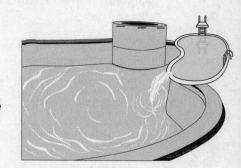

You can use a table of values and a coordinate plane to answer this question.

Recall that a **coordinate plane** is a system used to locate points represented along horizontal and vertical axes. An **ordered pair** (*x*, *y*) is a pair of numbers used to identify a point in the coordinate plane. In an ordered pair, the first coordinate, or **x-coordinate**, tells how far left or right horizontally the point is from the vertical axis. The second coordinate, or **y-coordinate**, tells how far up or down vertically the point is from the horizontal axis.

Here are some examples of ordered pairs that have been plotted on a coordinate plane.

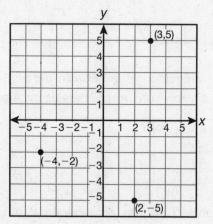

In many real world situations, only positive coordinates are needed since negative numbers don't apply to the situation. For example, relative to the swimming pool problem, only the first quadrant, where both the *x*- and *y*-coordinates are positive, should be shown on the coordinate plane.

Take It Apart

To answer the question, make a table of values. Then plot the pairs of values on a coordinate plane and connect them with a line.

Time (hr)	Depth (ft)	Point
1	2	(1, 2)
2	4	(2, 4)
3	6	(3, 6)
4	8	(4, 8)

Step 1 Use the rate to make a table of values. Write the pairs of values as points.

Step 2 Plot the points on the coordinate plane. In this problem, negative numbers don't make sense, so use only the first quadrant. Since time is the first coordinate in each point and depth is the second, label the horizontal axis "Number of Hours" and the vertical axis "Depth of Water". Plot each point carefully, moving first to the right and then up. Connect the dots with a line.

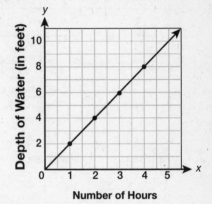

Step 3 Use the graph to determine when the depth will be 5 feet. To do this, find 5 feet on the vertical axis and trace over to the line you drew. Read the x-coordinate of the point.

The x-coordinate is $2\frac{1}{2}$.

Step 4 Answer the question.

Add 2 hours and 30 minutes to noon. The filter should be turned on at 2:30 P.M.

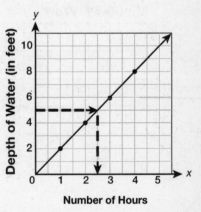

Use the strategy above to complete the table and plot the pairs of values on the coordinate plane.

Distance Traveled at a Rate of 50 km/hr

Time (hr)	Distance (km)	Point
1	50	
2	100	
3		
4		

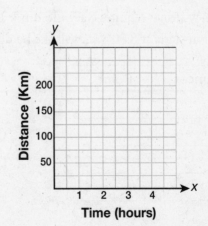

Lesson 5 **Plotting Pairs of Values on the Coordinate Plane**

Put It Together

Use what you now know about rates to complete the table of values for each situation and then plot the pairs of values on the coordinate plane. Be sure to label each axis properly.

1. Darren earns $6 for each hour he works.

Hours	Pay	Point
1		
2		
3		
4		

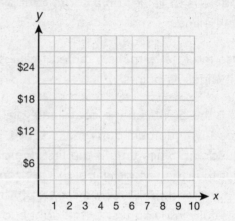

2. Keisha types 125 words every 4 minutes.

Minutes	Words	Point
4		
8		
12		
16		

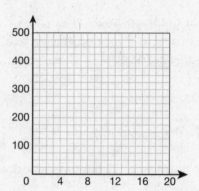

Complete the table and plot the pairs of values on the graph. Use the plot to find the answer.

3. A scan for kidney stones requires Karyn to drink at least 32 ounces of a liquid. She must drink 6 ounces every 5 minutes. If Karyn starts at 8:00 A.M., will she be done by 8:30? Use the plot to explain your answer.

Time	Ounces	Point
5		
10		
15		
20		

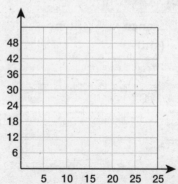

Make It Work

Answer the questions below.

1. A banana bread recipe calls for 2 cups of sugar for every 5 cups of flour. Which point would not be on a plot that describes this situation?

    A. (2, 5)

    B. (6, 15)

    C. (8, 20)

    D. (12, 25)

2. Joseph puts $3 out of every $10 that he earns in a box. If he were to plot pairs of values that describe this situation, which point would be on the plot?

    A. (20, 6)

    B. (30, 3)

    C. (13, 3)

    D. (13, 10)

3. The ratio of peanuts to almonds in a granola mix is 7 to 2. Write five points that you could plot on a coordinate plane to represent this situation.

_____

4. Chris hiked at a constant speed. He plotted pairs of values that represented the number of hours it took him to hike a certain number of miles. The pairs of values he plotted were: (2, 5), (4, 10), and (6, 15). Based on these pairs of values, at what rate did Chris hike in miles per hour?

_____

5. An architect built a model of a new apartment building. The building is 3 meters for every 4 centimeters of the model. Draw a graph and plot several pairs of values that could be used to calculate the conversion from the model to the building. Let the horizontal axis represent the model and the vertical axis represent the apartment building. Label the plot completely.

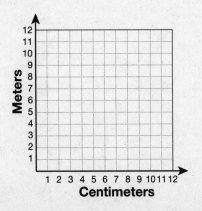

Lesson 6 · Solving Problems Involving Unit Rates

6.RP.3.b Solve unit rate problems including those involving unit pricing and constant speed. *For example, if it took 7 hours to mow 4 lawns, then at that rate, how many lawns could be mowed in 35 hours? At what rate were lawns being mowed?*

Real World Connections

Key Words

proportion

unit rate

A printer can print 5 pages of glossy color baseball cards in 8 minutes. At this rate, how many minutes will it take the printer to print 30 pages of baseball cards?

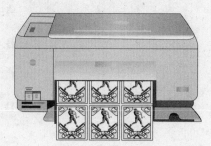

A **proportion** is an equation showing that two ratios are equal. For example, $\frac{3}{11} = \frac{15}{55}$ is a proportion since the two ratios are equal. In many problems, one of the terms in the proportion is missing. As long as you know three of the four terms, you can find the missing term using cross products.

A **unit rate** is a rate that has a denominator of 1. Recall that to find a unit rate, you can divide the numerator and the denominator by the denominator. Another method to find a unit rate is to write and solve a proportion. Consider this example. Dennis drove 560 miles in 14 hours. How many miles did he drive per hour? You could solve the proportion $\frac{560}{14} = \frac{?}{1}$ to find the answer.

Many real world problems involve rates and can be solved either by finding the unit rate or by writing and solving a proportion. You can use either method, but one is usually easier than the other, depending on the numbers in the problem. For example, if the unit rate is a whole number, then you may not need to write and solve a proportion.

Take It Apart

To write and solve a proportion, follow some simple steps.

Step 1 Read the problem carefully. Identify the rate given and the rate needed. Then write each rate as a fraction. Don't forget - you must keep the units in the same order.

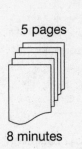

5 pages

8 minutes

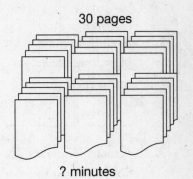

30 pages

? minutes

Given: 5 pages in 8 minutes $\longrightarrow \dfrac{5}{8}$

Needed: 30 pages in _____ minutes $\longrightarrow \dfrac{30}{?}$

Step 2 Write a proportion using the two rates.

$$\dfrac{5}{8} = \dfrac{30}{?}$$

Step 3 Now find the two cross products. Since the ratios form a proportion, the cross products must be equal.

$5 \times ? = 8 \times 30$
$5 \times ? = 240$

Step 4 Since the missing term is multiplied by 5, find its value by dividing by 5.

$240 \div 5 = 48$

Step 5 Answer the question using the missing term.

It will take the printer 48 minutes to print 30 pages of baseball cards.

Use the strategy above to answer each question. Label each answer with the appropriate unit.

1. Ginger made 16 free throws in 20 attempts. At this rate, how many free throws would she make in 50 attempts?

   _____

2. A motorist drove a constant speed of 56 miles per hour. How many miles did he drive in 4 hours?

   _____

3. Paul baked 12 pies in 8 hours. At this rate, how many pies can he bake in 20 hours?

   _____

4. Janice can type 4 pages in 15 minutes. At this rate, how long will it take her to type 24 pages?

   _____

Put It Together

Use what you now know about unit rates and proportions to answer each question.

1. Abdul can make 6 pizzas in 54 minutes. How long does it take him to make one pizza?

_____

2. A dozen Number 2 pencils cost $1.14. How much does 1 pencil cost?

_____

3. A machine makes 720 granola bars every 9 minutes. At this rate, how many granola bars will be made in 15 minutes?

_____

4. A water tank is being filled at a rate of 25 gallons every 15 minutes. If the tank holds 240 gallons and was completely empty, how many minutes will it take to fill the tank?

_____

Write a proportion for each situation. Then solve the proportion to answer the question.

5. Mrs. Chin wants to buy a rose for each of the girls in her sixth-grade class. She has $45 to spend. The sign at the flower shops says "A dozen roses for just $37." If there are 15 girls in Mrs. Chin's class, does she have enough money? Explain why or why not.

_____

_____

_____

6. Eva agreed to make 15 pies for the class bake sale. She bought 15 dozen apples to make the pies. She used 128 apples making the first 8 pies. At this rate, she will not have enough apples to make all 15 pies. How many more dozen apples should she buy? Explain how you found your answer.

_____

_____

_____

_____

Make It Work

Answer the questions below.

1. If it costs $82.50 to rent a kayak for 3 hours, how much does it cost to rent a kayak for 1 hour?

   A. $22.50

   B. $27.50

   C. $32.50

   D. $247.50

2. Isabella bought 4 CDs for $65. Each CD cost the same amount of money. At that rate, how much will she pay for 5 CDs?

   A. $52.00

   B. $75.00

   C. $78.50

   D. $81.25

3. Find the missing value in the proportion: $\frac{96}{6} = \frac{?}{20}$. Show your work.

   _____

4. Daisy raised $119 in two weeks for the sixth grade fundraiser. At this rate, how much can she expect to raise in 2 months? Explain how you found your answer.

   _____

   _____

5. During a drought, 3 inches of water evaporated from a large lake every 2 weeks. In a nearby town, 5 inches of water evaporated from a slightly smaller lake every 3 weeks. If these rates remain the same, how many more inches of water will have evaporated from the smaller lake than the larger lake after a total of 6 weeks? Justify your answer.

   _____

   _____

   _____

6.RP.3.c Find a percent of a quantity as a rate per 100 (e.g., 30% of a quantity means $\frac{30}{100}$ times the quantity); solve problems involving finding the whole, given a part and the percent.

Real World Connections

There are many real world connections to percents. Some examples are sale prices, markups, interest, commission, raises, and tips.

AnnMarie needs to buy a pack of tube socks for softball. She finds a pack that costs $8.00 and has a 25% off sticker. She finds another pack that she likes a little better for the same price, but it is not on sale. How much money will AnnMarie save if she buys the tube socks that are on sale?

To find a sale price, you need to know something about percents.

A **percent** (%) is a special type of ratio that compares a number to 100. The term *per cent* mean per hundred.

To find the percent of a quantity, write the percent as a rate per hundred and multiply by the quantity. It may make the multiplication easier if you write the quantity as a fraction with a denominator of 1. For example, 5% of 30 is $\frac{5}{100} \times \frac{30}{1} = \frac{150}{100} = 1.5$. It is also helpful to have a calculator handy, because some of the calculations may be tricky.

If you are given a part of a quantity and the percent, you can find the whole quantity by writing and solving a proportion that involves one ratio whose denominator is 100. Use this strategy to write the proportion: $\frac{\%}{100} = \frac{\text{part}}{\text{whole}}$. For example, if 40% of a quantity is 12, the proportion is $\frac{40}{100} = \frac{12}{?}$. Solve the proportion using cross products.

Toolbox

calculator

Key Word

percent

 Peoples Common Core Mathematics

Take It Apart

To find the percent of a quantity, follow some simple steps.

Step 1 Write the percent as a rate per hundred.

$$25\% = \frac{25}{100}$$

Step 2 Multiply the quantity by the rate. Remember, every whole number can be written as a fraction with a denominator of 1.

$$\frac{25}{100} \times \frac{8}{1} = \frac{200}{100} = 2$$

Step 3 Use your calculations to answer the question.

Since the pack of socks is 25% off and 25% of $8.00 is $2.00, AnnMarie will save $2.00 if she buys the pack that is on sale.

Use the strategy above to find the percent of the given quantity.

1. 10% of 65

_____

2. 25% of 48

_____

3. 20% of 140

_____

4. 75% of 200

_____

5. 16% of 16

_____

6. 1% of 500

_____

7. 2.5% of 80

_____

8. 150% of 36

_____

9. 200% of 140

_____

Lesson 7 · Using Rates to Solve Percent Problems

Put It Together

Use what you now know about percents to answer each question.

1. What is 45% of 120?

_____

2. The Coopers' food bill at a restaurant came to $76.00. How much should Mr. Cooper leave for a 15% tip?

_____

3. Thirty percent of a number is 24. Write and solve a proportion to find the number.

_____

4. A desk at a furniture store has been discounted 20% because it was slightly damaged. If the original price was $290, what is the amount of the discount?

_____

Answer each question. Show your work.

5. Francine has a collection of 25 dolls. If 12% of the dolls are China dolls, how many of the dolls are not China? Explain how you found your answer.

_____

_____

_____

_____

6. Luke got 88% of the questions on his math test correct. The number of questions he got correct was 22. How many questions were on the test? Justify your answer by writing and solving a proportion.

_____

_____

_____

Make It Work

Answer the questions below.

1. Gerard earns 3% annual interest on his $5,000 certificate of deposit. How much interest does he earn in 2 years?

   A. $15

   B. $30

   C. $150

   D. $300

2. Out of 100 customers, 36 made a purchase. What percent of the customers did not make a purchase?

   A. 36%

   B. 54%

   C. 64%

   D. 100%

3. Sixty percent of a number is 18. Write and solve a proportion to find the number. Show your work.

   _____

   _____

   _____

4. How much more would a 20% tip on an $82.00 food bill be than a 15% tip? Answer the question by finding each percent of $82 and comparing the results.

   _____

   _____

5. Explain in detail a different method to solve question 4 above. Then check to make sure the result is the same.

   _____

   _____

   _____

   _____

6.RP.3.d Use ratio reasoning to convert measurement units; manipulate and transform units appropriately when multiplying or dividing quantities.

Real World Connections

Key Word

conversion factor

Maria bought a 20-pound bag of dog food for Fido. She wants to divide it into 10-ounce packs so she can give Fido one pack per meal. How many packs will she have?

Before you can answer this question, you need to know how many ounces are in 20 pounds.

You can use ratios to convert measurement units. For example, since 1 foot = 12 inches, you can create a **conversion factor** from feet to inches in the form of a ratio. Actually, you can create two ratios, $\frac{1 \text{ foot}}{12 \text{ inches}}$ or $\frac{12 \text{ inches}}{1 \text{ foot}}$. Since the numerator and the denominator are equal in value, the ratio has a total value of 1. This means you can multiply any amount by one of these ratios and not change the actual amount.

Here is a table of some common conversions. Don't forget, you can abbreviate the units, as long as you use the standard abbreviations. For example, you can write *feet* as *ft*.

Conversion Factors in Ratio Form		
Length	**Weight**	**Capacity**
$\frac{1 \text{ foot}}{12 \text{ inches}}$ or $\frac{12 \text{ inches}}{1 \text{ foot}}$	$\frac{1 \text{ pound}}{16 \text{ ounces}}$ or $\frac{16 \text{ ounces}}{1 \text{ pound}}$	$\frac{1 \text{ gallon}}{4 \text{ quarts}}$ or $\frac{4 \text{ quarts}}{1 \text{ gallon}}$
$\frac{1 \text{ yard}}{3 \text{ feet}}$ or $\frac{3 \text{ feet}}{1 \text{ yard}}$	$\frac{1 \text{ ton}}{2,000 \text{ pounds}}$ or $\frac{2,000 \text{ pounds}}{1 \text{ ton}}$	$\frac{1 \text{ quart}}{2 \text{ pints}}$ or $\frac{2 \text{ pints}}{1 \text{ quart}}$
$\frac{1 \text{ mile}}{5,280 \text{ feet}}$ or $\frac{5,280 \text{ feet}}{1 \text{ mile}}$		$\frac{1 \text{ pint}}{2 \text{ cups}}$ or $\frac{2 \text{ cups}}{1 \text{ pint}}$

Here's a trick to help you remember which ratio to choose. The unit you <u>d</u>on't want to keep goes in the <u>d</u>enominator. Just remember the d's in <u>d</u>on't and <u>d</u>enominator. For example, if you want to convert gallons to quarts, you don't want to keep the unit gallons, so use the conversion factor $\frac{4 \text{ qt}}{1 \text{ gal}}$.

You can also use this strategy to convert units of time and metric units. For example, since 1,000 grams = 1 kilogram, two conversion factors are $\frac{1 \text{ kg}}{1,000 \text{ g}}$ or $\frac{1,000 \text{ g}}{1 \text{ kg}}$.

Take It Apart

To convert measurement units, follow some simple steps.

Step 1 Identify the units you have and the units you want.

Have: pounds   Want: ounces

Step 2 Choose the conversion factor (ratio), based on the two units. Be sure to choose the one that has the unit you <u>d</u>on't want to keep in the <u>d</u>enominator (remember the d's).

In this problem, you don't want to keep *pounds* so choose $\frac{16 \text{ ounces}}{1 \text{ pound}}$.

Step 3 Multiply the given quantity by the ratio. It may make the multiplication easier if you write the quantity over a denominator of $1\left(\frac{20 \text{ pounds}}{1}\right)$.

$$\frac{20 \text{ pounds}}{1} \times \frac{16 \text{ ounces}}{1 \text{ pound}} = \frac{20 \times 16 \text{ ounces}}{1} = 320 \text{ ounces}$$

There are 320 ounces in 20 pounds. (Notice that the units you didn't want to keep "cancelled" each other.)

Step 4 Use your converted measurement to answer the question.

Maria will have $320 \div 10 = 32$ ten-ounce packs of food.

Use the strategy above to convert each measurement to the indicated units.

1. 13 gallons to quarts

   _____

2. 96 inches to feet

   _____

3. 4.5 pounds to ounces

   _____

4. 126 yards to feet

   _____

 Chapter 1 • Ratio & Proportional Relationships **31**

Put It Together

Use what you now know about converting measurement units using ratios to answer each question.

1. An ice cream recipe calls for 3 pints of milk. How many cups is this?

2. Elise has 168 inches of ribbon. How many feet of ribbon does she have?

3. If 1 cup = 8 fluid ounces, how many cups equal 296 fluid ounces?

4. Which is longer, a 32-foot boat or a boat that has a length of 12 yards?

Write the conversion factor in ratio form needed to answer each question. Then answer the question.

5. If one bird weighs 8 ounces and each bird in a flock of 120 weighs the same, how many pounds does the whole flock of birds weigh?

6. Chad and Ramos picked strawberries all morning. At the end of the morning, they combined their strawberries. Chad had 22.5 pounds of strawberries and Ramos had 400 ounces. Explain how to determine the total weight of their strawberries. Then find the total weight in pounds.

Make It Work

Answer the questions below.

1. An elephant can weigh as much as 15,000 pounds. How many tons could an elephant weigh?

   A. 7.5   B. 15.5

   C. 70.5   D. 150.5

2. There are 10 millimeters in 1 centimeter. How many centimeters are there in 5 millimeters?

   A. $\frac{1}{2}$ B. 2

   C. 5   D. 50

3. Lila has 2.5 feet of ribbon for wrapping packages. She uses 14 inches of ribbon on the first package she wraps. How many inches of ribbon does she have left? Explain how you found your answer.

   _____

   _____

   _____

4. Explain how to convert 7 yards to inches using two ratios as conversion factors. Then do the conversion.

   _____

   _____

   _____

5. Marian is buying bottles of lemonade for a family reunion. The lemonade is sold in 1-quart bottles. Fifty-six people are attending the reunion, and Marian would like every person to be able to have 3 cups of lemonade. How many 1-quart bottles of lemonade does Marian need to buy? Describe the steps you used to solve the problem.

   _____

   _____

   _____

Question 1: Where did pi (π) come from?

The number pi (π) has a value of just slightly more than 3. It is used to find the area and circumference of a circle. But where did it come from?

Thousands of years ago, mathematicians discovered that the *ratio* of every circle's circumference to its diameter was approximately 3 to 1. They worked very hard to find an even more precise value of this ratio and eventually arrived at 3.14 to 1. The common value for π is now accepted to be 3.14, even though we know it is not an exact value.

To convince yourself that all these mathematicians were correct, try finding the ratio of the circumference of different size circles to their diameters. You can do this using a compass, a ruler, and a piece of string.

Step 1 Draw a dot for the center of a circle and use your compass to carefully draw the circle.

Step 2 Measure the diameter of the circle with your ruler. Don't forget—you must measure through the center that you marked. Round to the nearest quarter of an inch.

Step 3 Carefully lay a piece of string around the edge of the circle until it meets. Then measure its length. Round to the nearest quarter of an inch.

Step 4 Write the ratio of the circumference to the diameter and confirm that it is approximately equivalent to 3.14 to 1. Remember, the cross products of two equivalent ratios will be the same when you write the ratios as a proportion.

Question 2: Which is the better buy?

When you go to the grocery store, it is very common to see different size packages for almost everything you can buy. For example, many cereals come in small and large boxes; peanut butter comes in small and large jars; and bottled water comes in packs of different numbers of bottles. To truly determine which is the better buy, you must consider the unit price, which is the price per one unit of the product. The unit depends on the product, but is usually in ounces for most grocery items.

So, try this. Go to the store and pick a specific cereal that comes in two different sizes. Write down the price and the number of ounces in each box. Then determine which is the better buy by finding the unit price. Repeat this exercise for several items, such as peanut butter, soda, water, etc.

Compare your results to some of your classmates'. Is it always the bigger package that is the better buy?

When you get older and start buying your own groceries, trust me, you'll find this to be a very useful skill.

Question 3: How much should we tip?

Wouldn't you like to be able to tell your mom or dad how much they should tip when you eat at a restaurant? The current tipping rates are 15% for acceptable service and 20% for really good service. Let's create a "cheat sheet" for calculating tips.

Create a 3-column table. The first column should be a list of prices ranging from $40 to $100 in increments of $5. The middle column will be for a 15% tip and the last column for a 20% tip. Work with a partner and use what you learned about ratios to calculate the tips for each price and record them in your table.

Then come up with a strategy for how you might "guesstimate" the tips for values in between the prices in your table. For example, how much tip would you leave for a $52 meal based on you calculations for a $50 meal and a $55 meal? Share your strategy with your classmates.

Question 4: Wait! How fast is that?

Did you know that almost every country outside of the United States uses metric measurements? So, if you visit a foreign country, the speed limit signs might look like they belong on a racetrack. This is because the speed is posted in kilometers per hour rather than miles per hour, and a kilometer is much shorter than a mile. In fact, the ratio 0.62 to 1 shows the relationship between a kilometer and a mile. This ratio can be used to convert kilometers to miles.

Use the Internet to research 10 different countries to find the most common highway speed limits. Highways are also called freeways, expressways, or motorways. Then use the ratio for converting kilometers to miles to write the equivalent speed limit that you would see in the United States.

Compare your results to those of your classmates. Which 3 countries have the highest speed limits?

Actually, did you know that some countries don't have any speed limits at all on their highways? That might not be the best idea!

6.NS.1 Interpret and compute quotients of fractions, and solve word problems involving division of fractions by fractions, e.g., by using visual fraction models and equations to represent the problem. *For example, create a story context for $\left(\frac{2}{3}\right) \div \left(\frac{3}{4}\right)$ and use a visual fraction model to show the quotient; use the relationship between multiplication and division to explain that $\left(\frac{2}{3}\right) \div \left(\frac{3}{4}\right) = \frac{8}{9}$ because $\frac{3}{4}$ of $\frac{8}{9}$ is $\frac{2}{3}$. (In general, $\left(\frac{a}{b}\right) \div \left(\frac{c}{d}\right) = \frac{ad}{bc}$.) How much chocolate will each person get if 3 people share $\frac{1}{2}$ lb of chocolate equally? How many $\frac{3}{4}$-cup servings are in $\frac{2}{3}$ of a cup of yogurt? How wide is a rectangular strip of land with length $\frac{3}{4}$ mi and area $\frac{1}{2}$ square mi?*

Real World Connections

You're helping to bake brownies for your club bake sale, but you are very low on salt. You have only $\frac{1}{3}$ teaspoon of salt. Each batch uses $\frac{1}{8}$ teaspoon. How many batches of brownies can you make?

In this situation, you need to be able to find the quotient of two fractions. A **quotient** is the result of dividing one number by another number. The number that you divide by is the **divisor**. If you need to share a pizza among three people, then 3 is your divisor.

When you divide by a fraction, you can find your answer by multiplying by the reciprocal of your divisor. **Reciprocals** are two numbers that have a product of 1. For example, $\frac{2}{3}$ and $\frac{3}{2}$ are reciprocals because $\frac{2}{3} \times \frac{3}{2} = \frac{6}{6} = 1$. Likewise, the reciprocal of 3 is $\frac{1}{3}$ because $3 \times \frac{1}{3} = \frac{3}{3} = 1$.

You can use multiplication to help check that your answer is correct. When you multiply the quotient by the divisor, you should get your original number.

Toolbox

calculator

Key Words

quotient

divisor

reciprocals

Peoples Common Core Mathematics

Take It Apart

To divide fractions, follow some simple steps.

Step 1 Write the division expression using fractions.

$$\frac{1}{3} \div \frac{1}{8}$$

Step 2 Write the reciprocal of the divisor by switching its numerator and denominator.

The reciprocal of $\frac{1}{8}$ is $\frac{8}{1}$.

Step 3 Rewrite the division expression as a multiplication expression using the reciprocal.

$$\frac{1}{3} \div \frac{1}{8} = \frac{1}{3} \times \frac{8}{1}$$

Step 4 Find the product. Write the answer in simplest form.

$$\frac{1}{3} \div \frac{1}{8} = \frac{1}{3} \times \frac{8}{1} = \frac{8}{3} = 2\frac{2}{3}$$

You have enough salt to make 2 batches of brownies.

Multiplying by the reciprocal is also helpful when dividing by a whole number. Just remember that a whole number can be written as a fraction that has 1 as the denominator.

Divide $\frac{1}{2}$ liter of soft drink among 5 people.

$$\frac{1}{2} \div 5 = \frac{1}{2} \div \frac{5}{1} = \frac{1}{2} \times \frac{1}{5} = \frac{1}{10}$$

Each person gets $\frac{1}{10}$ liter of soft drink.

Use the strategy above to find the quotient for each of these problems. Show your work. Use multiplication to check your answers.

1. $\frac{2}{5} \div \frac{4}{7}$

_____

2. $\frac{12}{13} \div 4$

_____

Put It Together

Use what you now know about dividing by fractions to find the following quotients. Write your answer in simplest form. Show your work.

1. $\frac{5}{3} \div \frac{5}{7}$

2. $\frac{2}{7} \div \frac{4}{13}$

3. $\frac{4}{9} \div \frac{5}{6}$

_____

_____

_____

4. $\frac{6}{7} \div 8$

5. $\frac{2}{5} \div 4$

6. $\frac{5}{14} \div 15$

_____

_____

_____

Answer the questions. Share your ideas with a classmate.

7. Use multiplication to show whether $\frac{14}{15} \div \frac{14}{9} = \frac{1}{5}$ is correct.

_____

_____

8. How does the reciprocal of a reciprocal compare with the original number? Give an example to support your answer.

_____

_____

_____

Make It Work

Answer the questions below.

1. What is the quotient of $\frac{21}{32} \div \frac{3}{4}$?

   A. $1\frac{1}{7}$

   B. $1\frac{13}{32}$

   C. $\frac{7}{8}$

   D. $\frac{63}{128}$

2. What is the quotient of $\frac{8}{18} \div 12$?

   A. $\frac{3}{16}$

   B. $\frac{1}{27}$

   C. $5\frac{1}{3}$

   D. 27

3. Describe the process of finding the quotient of two fractions using the terms *quotient*, *reciprocal*, and *divisor*.

   _____

   _____

4. A student wants to check his solution to the problem $\frac{1}{2} \div \frac{3}{4} = \frac{2}{3}$ by multiplying $\frac{1}{2} \times \frac{2}{3}$. Analyze whether his method will work and offer corrections if needed.

   _____

   _____

   _____

5. Two students are preparing bags of popcorn for movie night. They must prepare 12 bags of popcorn from a larger bag containing 5 pounds of popcorn. Joan suggests dividing 5 pounds by 12. Carlos suggests multiplying 5 pounds by $\frac{1}{12}$. Analyze each student's solution.

   _____

   _____

   _____

Lesson 10 Solving Word Problems Involving the Division of Fractions

6.NS.1 Interpret and compute quotients of fractions, and solve word problems involving division of fractions by fractions, e.g., by using visual fraction models and equations to represent the problem.

For example, create a story context for $(\frac{2}{3}) \div (\frac{3}{4})$ and use a visual fraction model to show the quotient; use the relationship between multiplication and division to explain that $(\frac{2}{3}) \div (\frac{3}{4}) = \frac{8}{9}$ because $\frac{3}{4}$ of $\frac{8}{9}$ is $\frac{2}{3}$. (In general, $(\frac{a}{b}) \div (\frac{c}{d}) = \frac{ad}{bc}$.) How much chocolate will each person get if 3 people share $\frac{1}{2}$ lb of chocolate equally? How many $\frac{3}{4}$-cup servings are in $\frac{2}{3}$ of a cup of yogurt? How wide is a rectangular strip of land with length $\frac{3}{4}$ mi and area $\frac{1}{2}$ square mi?

Real World Connections

Toolbox

calculator

Key Words

quotient

divisor

reciprocals

You go to a restaurant that serves a $\frac{1}{2}$-pound hamburger. However, the recommended serving size is $\frac{1}{4}$ pound. How many servings does the hamburger provide?

In this situation, you need to be able to solve a problem by finding the quotient of two fractions. A **quotient** is the result of dividing one number by another number. The number that you divide by is the **divisor**.

You may remember that when you divide by a fraction, you can find your answer by multiplying by the reciprocal of your divisor. **Reciprocals** are two numbers that have a product of 1. For example, $\frac{2}{3}$ and $\frac{3}{2}$ are reciprocals because $\frac{2}{3} \times \frac{3}{2} = 1$.

You can also divide fractions by drawing models to represent the problem.

Take It Apart

To solve a word problem that involves dividing fractions, follow some simple steps.

Step 1   Determine an expression for the problem you need to solve.

You need to find how many $\frac{1}{4}$-pound servings make up a $\frac{1}{2}$-pound hamburger. $\frac{1}{2} \div \frac{1}{4}$.

Step 2   Divide the fractions by showing fraction bars for the fractions that you are dividing.

Draw two equal length rectangles. Divide one of them into two bars and the other into four bars.

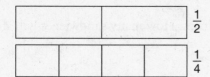

Step 3   Determine how many pieces of the divisor are needed to equal the original number.

Two $\frac{1}{4}$ bars equal a $\frac{1}{2}$ bar.

Step 4   Report your answer.

$\frac{1}{2} \div \frac{1}{4} = 2$ The $\frac{1}{2}$-pound hamburger provides 2 servings of $\frac{1}{4}$ pound each.

When dividing a whole number by a fraction, draw rectangles to represent the whole number. Then, divide each rectangle into bars based on the denominator of the divisor. Finally, count the number of divisor models shown.

Use the strategy above to finish solving these problems.

1. A carpenter has a board that is $\frac{3}{5}$-yard long. She wants to cut pieces that are $\frac{3}{10}$-yard long. How many $\frac{3}{10}$-yard pieces can she cut from the board?

$\frac{3}{5} \div \frac{3}{10} = $ _____

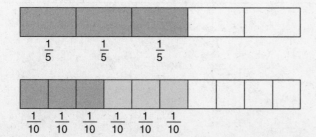

Put It Together

Use your tools and what you now know about solving word problems that involve dividing fractions to find each quotient.

1. A runner sets a goal to run 60 miles. How many days will it take to reach the goal if he runs $\frac{3}{4}$ mile each day?

   _____

2. How many $\frac{1}{20}$-meter lengths of rope can be cut from a rope that is $\frac{4}{5}$-meter long?

   _____

3. Mariah orders a 6-foot sub for a party and cuts it into $\frac{1}{4}$-foot sandwiches. How many sandwiches will she have?

   _____

4. A rug has an area of $\frac{1}{2}$ square yard. If the rug is $\frac{1}{3}$-yard long, how wide is it?

   _____

Answer the questions. Share your ideas with a classmate.

5. Write the quotient if you divide $\frac{a}{b}$ by $\frac{c}{d}$. Explain your work.

   _____

6. A student began a problem by drawing the model shown. Based on the model, what can you tell about the numbers in the problem being solved?

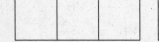 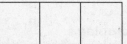  

   _____

   _____

   _____

Make It Work

Answer the questions below.

1. How many $\frac{3}{4}$-cup portions are in $\frac{1}{2}$ cup of juice?

   A. $\frac{3}{8}$

   B. $\frac{1}{3}$

   C. $\frac{2}{3}$

   D. $2\frac{2}{3}$

2. Which of the following problems does the model best represent?

   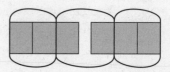

   A. How many $\frac{1}{3}$-pound servings are in 2 pounds of popcorn?

   B. How many $\frac{1}{6}$-pound servings are in 2 pounds of popcorn?

   C. How many $\frac{3}{4}$-pound servings are in 2 pounds of popcorn?

   D. How many $\frac{2}{3}$-pound servings are in 2 pounds of popcorn?

3. How many $\frac{2}{3}$-pound servings of dog food are in a $4\frac{1}{3}$-pound bag?

   _____

4. Cody wants to divide $\frac{7}{8}$ cup of rice into $\frac{1}{3}$-cup containers. How many containers does he need? Explain how you found your answer.

   _____

5. A recipe makes 3 dozen cookies using $\frac{3}{4}$ cup brown sugar. An order is placed for 9 dozen cookies. Will the baker need to get more brown sugar to complete the order if there is only $2\frac{1}{2}$ cups in the bakery? Explain how you found your answer.

   _____

   _____

   _____

6.NS.2   Fluently divide multi-digit numbers using the standard algorithm.

Real World Connections

You are helping to pack confetti eggs into cartons to sell at the school carnival. You have egg cartons that can hold 12 eggs each. You need to figure out how many egg cartons you will need to hold 259 eggs.

You can use division to find out how many groups of objects you have or how many objects are in each group. In this case, you are looking for how many groups of 12 eggs you have in 259 eggs.

If your **dividend,** the number you are dividing, is a multiple of your divisor, you will get a quotient that is a whole number with nothing left over. However, if your dividend is not a multiple of your divisor, you will have an amount left over. The **remainder** is the amount left over after finding the quotient. The remainder is always less than the divisor.

Key Words

dividend

remainder

Take It Apart

To divide two whole numbers, follow some simple steps.

Step 1   Divide. Decide where to put the first digit of the quotient. Determine what number to use based on what will multiply by the divisor and still be less than or equal to the value in the dividend.

$$
\begin{array}{r}
21 \\
12\overline{)259} \\
-24\downarrow \\
\hline
19 \\
-12 \\
\hline
7
\end{array}
$$

There are not enough hundreds to divide by 12, but you can divide 25 tens by 12. Place the number 2 in the quotient above the tens place because $12 \times 2 < 25$.

Peoples Common Core Mathematics

Step 2   Multiply and subtract. Multiply the number that you placed in the quotient by the divisor. Subtract the result from the dividend.

$2 \times 12 = 24; 25 - 24 = 1$

Step 3   Bring down the next digit. Repeat the process of dividing, multiplying, subtracting, and bringing down a digit until you have divided all the digits of the dividend by the divisor.

$1 \times 12 = 12; 19 - 12 = 7$

Step 4   If the final difference is not zero, then you have a remainder. Write this number at the end of the quotient following the letter R.

You will need 22 egg cartons. You will fill 21 cartons and have only 7 eggs in the last carton.

Use the strategy above to complete each problem and find each quotient.

1.

2. $41\overline{)492}$
     $-\square\downarrow$
      $\square 2$
     $-\square$
      $\square$

Put It Together

Use your tools and what you now know about dividing whole numbers to find the quotient for each of the following problems.

1. $43\overline{)172}$

2. $34\overline{)2,568}$

3. $12\overline{)1,564}$

4. $338 \div 26$

5. $5,546 \div 12$

6. $510 \div 34$

Answer the questions. Share your ideas with a classmate.

7. There are 295 students in sixth grade at Central Middle School who must take science. The maximum number of students in a science class is 22. How many science classes must be planned? Explain your work.

_____

_____

_____

8. Explain why the remainder must always be less than the divisor.

_____

_____

_____

Make It Work

Answer the questions below.

1. Keiran wants to save $56 for a gift for his mother's birthday in 14 weeks. How much money must he save each week?

   A. $0.25

   B. $4

   C. $5

   D. $8

2. Which of the following expressions is equal to 15?

   A. 225 ÷ 15

   B. 150 ÷ 15

   C. 168 ÷ 12

   D. 425 ÷ 15

3. A school science fair has 24 projects about earth science and 36 projects about physical science. The projects will be displayed in separate rows with an equal number of projects in each row. If there are 10 rows, how many projects will be in each row?

   _____

4. Joaquin has to read a 252-page book in 6 weeks. If he reads only 6 days each week, how many pages per day must he read? Explain your work.

   _____

   _____

   _____

5. Students will be riding on buses for a field trip to a science museum. There are 210 students and 10 teachers who will be going. How many buses will be needed if each bus can hold 44 people? Could fewer buses be used if the school uses larger buses that each hold 52 people? Explain your reasoning.

   _____

   _____

   _____

Lesson 12 — Adding and Subtracting Multi-Digit Decimals

6.NS.3 Fluently add, subtract, multiply, and divide multi-digit decimals using the standard algorithm for each operation.

Real World Connections

Key Words

decimal

sum

difference

You are loading your backpack at the end of school. You are bringing home your math and science books. You also have a binder that is filled with papers and a pencil case with all of your pens, pencils, and calculator. As you struggle to lift your backpack, you think it must weigh a ton. But just how heavy is it?

Imagine that your math book weighs 3.65 pounds, your science book weighs 3.93 pounds, your binder weighs 2.9 pounds, and your pencil case weighs 0.5 pound. You can use addition of decimals to find the total weight of your backpack.

A **decimal** is a number that has one or more digits to the right of the decimal point. When adding or subtracting decimals you must first line up the decimal points. The answer to an addition problem is called the **sum**. The answer to a subtraction problem is called the **difference**.

Take It Apart

To add or subtract decimals, follow some simple steps.

Step 1 Align the decimal points. Use zero as a placeholder if necessary.

Because 2.9 pounds and 0.5 pounds end in the tenths place, use zero as a placeholder in each number to help the digits align correctly.

$$
\begin{array}{r}
\overset{2}{3}.65 \\
3.93 \\
2.90 \\
+\,0.50 \\
\hline
10.98
\end{array}
$$

Step 2 Add or subtract the digits in each column, from right to left. Regroup as needed.

Step 3 Write the decimal point in the answer so that it lines up with the decimal points in the problem.

The total weight you are carrying home in your backpack is 10.98 pounds. Keep your work neat so that you can easily place the decimal point in the correct place in your answer.

What if you clean out your binder and remove 1.2 pounds of old papers? Then your backpack would weigh only 9.78 pounds.

$$
\begin{array}{r}
10.98 \\
-1.20 \\
\hline
9.78
\end{array}
$$

Use the strategy above to complete each problem and find each sum or difference.

1. $\begin{array}{r} 12.67 \\ +1.65 \\ \hline \end{array}$

2. $\begin{array}{r} 72.2 \\ -3.56 \\ \hline \end{array}$

3. $1.25 + 14.6 + 9.45$

   _____

Lesson 12 **Adding and Subtracting Multi-Digit Decimals**

Put It Together

Use your tools and what you now know about adding and subtracting decimals to find the following sums and differences.

1. 172.6
    + 21.45
    _____

2. 21.67
    + 431.598
    _____

3. 1,465.78
      − 41.4
    _____

4. 338.87 − 13.6

    _____

5. 5.545 + 12.12

    _____

6. 51.07 − 34.45

    _____

Answer the questions. Share your ideas with a classmate.

7. Why can you add zero at the end of a decimal without changing the value of the number?

    _____

    _____

    _____

    _____

8. The sum of 122 + 23 is 145. Why is the sum of 1.22 + 2.3 not 1.45?

    _____

    _____

    _____

Make It Work

Answer the questions below.

1. A puppy that weighed 1.62 pounds now weighs 20.4 pounds. How much weight has the puppy gained?

   A.   4.2 pounds

   B.   18.78 pounds

   C.   20.4 pounds

   D.   22.02 pounds

2. Which is the sum of 56.8 + 4.35 + 120?

   A.   73.15

   B.   181.15

   C.   220.3

   D.   1,123

3. Tanya has 14.78 feet of yarn. She cuts a piece 3.5 feet long and a second piece 5.6 feet long. What is the length of the remaining piece?

   _____

4. A student is testing the effect of different waters on plant growth. Plant A is 13.45 inches tall. Plant B is 1.2 inches taller than Plant A. Plant C is 2.1 inches shorter than Plant B. What is the height of the shortest plant? Which plant is the shortest?

   _____

5. You buy a book for $10.99 and pay $0.91 in sales tax. How much change should you receive from a $20 bill? Explain your work.

   _____

   _____

   _____

6.NS.3   Fluently add, subtract, multiply, and divide multi-digit decimals using the standard algorithm
for each operation.

Real World Connections

You're helping to prepare bags of grapes
for a mobile food pantry. You wash 11 bags
of grapes. Each bag holds 3.25 pounds of
grapes. Then you divide the grapes into
0.25-pound portions. At the end of the day,
you wonder how many pounds of grapes
you washed and how many bags you filled.

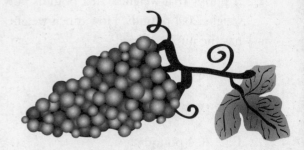

You can use multiplication and division of decimals to find the answers to these
questions. A **decimal** is a number that has one or more digits to the right of the
decimal point. When multiplying decimals, you do not need to line up the decimal
points. For multiplication, you count the number of digits to the right of the
decimal point in each factor. A **factor** is a number that you multiply. The answer to
a multiplication problem is called the **product**. The total number of digits to the
right of the decimal point in the factors equals the number of digits to the right of
the decimal point in the product.

If you are dividing by a decimal, you must first change the divisor to a whole
number. You adjust the dividend by the same power of 10. The answer to a
division problem is called the **quotient**. The decimal point in the quotient will be
lined up with the decimal point in the dividend.

Take It Apart

To multiply decimals, follow some simple steps.

Step 1 Multiply the factors as you would with whole numbers.

Step 2 Count the number of digits to the right of the decimal point in each factor.

There are 2 digits to the right of the decimal point in 3.25 and none in 11.

```
   3.25
 ×   11
   325
+ 3250
  35.75
```

Step 3 Place the decimal point in the product. You should have the same number of digits to the right of the decimal point as the total number of digits you counted in the factors.

The product should have 2 digits to the right of the decimal point.
You washed 35.75 pounds of grapes.

To divide decimals, follow some simple steps.

Step 1 Change the divisor to a whole number by multiplying it by a power of 10. Multiply the dividend by the same power of 10.

Change 0.25 to the whole number 25 by multiplying by 100. Change 35.75 to 3, 575 by multiplying by 100.

```
0.25)35.75
        143
 25)3575
   − 25↓↓
      107↓
    − 100↓
        75
      −  75
         0
```

Step 2 Divide as you do with whole numbers.

Step 3 Place the decimal point in the quotient directly above the decimal point in the dividend.

Placing the decimal point in the quotient above its position in the dividend shows that you filled 143 bags of grapes.

Use the strategy above to complete each problem and find each product or quotient.

1. 15.86 × 2.44

2. 18.688 ÷ 1.46

3. 20.774 ÷ 15.98

_____   _____   _____

Put It Together

Use your tools and what you now know about multiplying and dividing decimals to find the following products and quotients.

1. 72.64
    × 21.45
    _____

2. 21.67
    × 4.5
    _____

3. 1.24)‾56.6432‾
    _____

4. 338.912 ÷ 13.6
    _____

5. 45.5 × 1.12
    _____

6. 68.7 ÷ 34.35
    _____

Answer the questions. Share your ideas with a classmate.

7. If a factor is a decimal, can the product have fewer digits to the right of the decimal than the factor has? Provide an example.

    _____

    _____

    _____

    _____

8. You multiply the divisor by 10 to change it to a whole number but then forget to multiply the dividend by 10 before you divide. How will your answer compare to the correct answer?

    _____

    _____

Make It Work

Answer the questions below.

1. Which of the following products will have 3 digits to the right of the decimal point?

   A. 1.2 × 4.5

   B. 6.32 × 1.37

   C. 2.673 × 1.323

   D. 3.4 × 1.26

2. Which of the following quotients is the greatest?

   A. 30.75 ÷ 1.23

   B. 3.075 ÷ 12.3

   C. 0.3075 ÷ 0.123

   D. 307.5 ÷ 123

3. Giorgio worked 24.75 hours and earned $186.87. How much does he earn per hour?

   _____

4. Compare the cost per ounce for cereal if a 14.5-ounce box costs $2.76 and a 36.5-ounce box costs $7.30.

   _____

   _____

   _____

5. What area does a rug that is 3.45 feet wide and 6.65 feet long cover? What is the length of a rug that has the same area but is 4.75 feet wide?

   _____

Lesson 14 Finding the Greatest Common Factor

6.NS.4 Find the greatest common factor of two whole numbers less than or equal to 100 and the least common multiple of two whole numbers less than or equal to 12. Use the distributive property to express a sum of two whole numbers 1–100 with a common factor as a multiple of a sum of two whole numbers with no common factor. *For example, express 36 + 8 as 4 (9 + 2).*

Real World Connections

You are helping to wrap gifts for a local charity. You are given ribbon in two lengths. The pink pieces are 36 inches long, and the blue are 48 inches long.

You are asked to cut the ribbon so that all the pieces are the same length without wasting any of the ribbon.

Key Word

greatest common factor (GCF)

To solve this problem, you need to find the greatest number that will divide evenly into both 36 and 48. In other words, you need to find the greatest common factor of these numbers. The **greatest common factor (GCF)** is the greatest whole number that is a factor of two or more numbers.

The greatest common factor can be used along with the distributive property to express the sum of two numbers. The total length of the pieces of ribbon can be expressed using the length of each piece that you cut (the greatest common factor) distributed over the number of pieces of ribbon that you cut from each color.

 ## Take It Apart

To find the greatest common factor of two numbers, follow some simple steps.

Step 1 List all the factors for each number in order from least to greatest.

Factors of 36: 1, 2, 3, 4, 6, 9, 12, 18, 36

Factors of 48: 1, 2, 3, 4, 6, 8, 12, 16, 24, 48

Step 2 Find all common factors.

Common factors for 36 and 48: 1, 2, 3, 4, 6, 12

Step 3 Find the greatest number that is a common factor.

The greatest factor that 36 and 48 have in common is 12. So, you should cut the ribbon into 12-inch lengths.

To use the greatest common factor and the distributive property to express the sum of two numbers, follow some simple steps.

Step 1 Find the greatest common factor.

The GCF of 36 and 48 is 12.

Step 2 Divide the GCF into each number that you are adding.

Because $36 \div 12 = 3$ and $48 \div 12 = 4$, the problem $36 + 48$ can be rewritten as $12(3 + 4)$. Notice that this sum reflects the length of each ribbon that you cut (12 inches) and the number of pieces that you cut from the two ribbons (3 pink + 4 blue).

Use the strategy above to complete each problem involving a greatest common factor.

1. What is the greatest common factor of 18 and 42?

   Factors of 18: _____

   Factors of 42: _____

   GCF of 18 and 42: _____

2. How can $18 + 42$ be expressed using the GCF and the distributive property?

   GCF of 18 and 42: _____

   $18 + 42 =$ _____

Put It Together

Use what you now know about greatest common factors to find the GCF of each pair of numbers.

1. 15 and 25

2. 66 and 99

3. 81 and 36

Use what you now know about greatest common factors to express each sum using the distributive property.

4. 46 + 36

5. 64 + 40

6. 14 + 49

Answer the questions. Share your ideas with a classmate.

7. When is the GCF of a pair of numbers one of the numbers?

8. While practicing expressing sums using greatest common factors and the distributive property, a student wrote the following expression: 6(12 + 16). Analyze this expression and suggest how to improve it.

Make It Work

Answer the questions below.

1. Which of the following pairs of numbers has 12 as the greatest common factor?

   A. 24 and 48

   B. 12 and 18

   C. 6 and 4

   D. 36 and 48

2. Which of the following expressions correctly shows the use of the distributive property with the greatest common factor for the addition of 36 + 54?

   A. $2(18 + 27)$

   B. $3(12 + 18)$

   C. $18(2 + 3)$

   D. $36(1 + 18)$

3. A school science fair has 24 projects about earth science and 36 projects about physical science. The projects will be displayed in separate rows by subject with an equal number of projects in each row. Which is the greatest number of projects that can be in a row?

   _____

4. You are making bags of trail mix for a camping trip. You have 48 ounces of peanuts and 20 ounces of cashews. You need to have the same amount of each type of nut in each bag. Which is the maximum number of bags that you can make? How many ounces of each nut will be in each bag? Express the sum of nuts using the distributive property to support your answer.

   _____

   _____

   _____

5. The greatest common factor of a two-digit number and 8 is 2. The number has the digit 6 in the ones place. What are the possible values of the two-digit number? Explain your work.

   _____

   _____

   _____

Lesson 15 Finding the Least Common Multiple

6.NS.4 Find the greatest common factor of two whole numbers less than or equal to 100 and the least common multiple of two whole numbers less than or equal to 12. Use the distributive property to express a sum of two whole numbers 1–100 with a common factor as a multiple of a sum of two whole numbers with no common factor. *For example, express 36 + 8 as 4 (9 + 2).*

Real World Connections

You are shopping for a party and are picking up hot dogs and hot dog buns. You want to be sure that every hot dog can be served in a bun. You pick up a 10-pack of hot dogs. But when you get a package of hot dog buns, you see that the buns are sold in packs of 8. What is the fewest number of hot dogs and buns you need to buy so that every hot dog has a bun and nothing is left over?

To solve the problem of getting equal numbers of hot dogs and buns, you need to find a multiple that the numbers share. A **multiple** of a number is the product of the number and any whole number greater than zero. A **common multiple** of two or more numbers is a number that is a multiple of each of those numbers. It is a multiple that the numbers share, or have in common. The **least common multiple (LCM)** is the least number that is a common multiple of two or more numbers. To buy the fewest hot dogs and hot dog buns, you need to find the least common multiple of 10 and 8.

Take It Apart

To find the least common multiple of two numbers, follow some simple steps.

Step 1 Write the first ten multiples of each number. Multiply each number by the counting numbers 1 through 10.

The first ten multiples of 10: 10, 20, 30, **40**, 50, 60, 70, **80**, 90, 100

The first ten multiples of 8: 8, 16, 24, 32, **40**, 48, 56, 64, 72, **80**

Step 2 Find the numbers that are common to both lists. These are common multiples.

Common multiples of 10 and 8 are 40 and 80.

Step 3 Choose the least common multiple.

The least common multiple (LCM) of 10 and 8 is 40. You would need to buy 40 hot dogs and 40 hot dog buns for each hot dog to be served in a bun.

To find the number of packs of each item that you need, divide the least common multiple by the number of items in each pack.

40 hot dogs ÷ 10 hot dogs/pack = 4 packs of hot dogs

40 hot dog buns ÷ 8 hot dog buns/pack = 5 packs of hot dog buns

Use the strategy above to complete each problem and find each least common multiple.

1. Find the least common multiple of 4 and 6.

   Multiples of 4: _____

   Multiples of 6: _____

   Common multiples: _____

   Least common multiple: _____

2. Find the least common multiple of 5 and 7.

   Multiples of 5: _____

   Multiples of 7: _____

   Common multiples: _____

   Least common multiple: _____

Put It Together

Use what you now know about least common multiples to find the LCM of each pair of numbers.

1. 2 and 9

_____

2. 4 and 8

_____

3. 9 and 12

_____

Use what you now know about least common multiples to solve the following problems.

4. While shopping for school supplies, you see that pencils are sold in packs of 12 and pens are sold in packs of 10. What is the least number of pens and pencils you could buy to have an equal number of each?

_____

5. Eggs are sold by the dozen, but biscuits are sold in packs of 8. What is the least number of eggs and of biscuits you could buy to have an equal number of each?

_____

Answer the questions. Share your ideas with a classmate.

6. When is the LCM of a pair of numbers one of the numbers?

_____

_____

7. Describe how you could find the least common multiple of two numbers by writing out the multiples of just the larger number instead of writing out the multiples of both numbers.

_____

_____

_____

       Peoples Common Core Mathematics

Make It Work

Answer the questions below.

1. For which pair of numbers is 24 the least common multiple?

   A. 2 and 12

   B. 3 and 4

   C. 4 and 6

   D. 6 and 8

2. Which pair of numbers has the same least common multiple as 3 and 10?

   A. 2 and 5

   B. 5 and 6

   C. 5 and 10

   D. 8 and 3

3. You are the eighteenth person in line at a grand opening of a store. Every sixth person receives a $5 gift card, and every eighth person receives a free shirt. What gift will you receive? How many places from your position will be the first to receive both gifts?

_____

_____

4. A plumber is hired to stop leaks in a bathroom. The faucet drips every 6 seconds. The shower drips every 9 seconds. If both fixtures just dripped, how long will it be before they both drip at the same time again? Explain your work.

_____

_____

_____

5. You are preparing breakfast platters for Teacher Appreciation Week. You are serving an equal number of muffins and bagels. The muffins come in packs of 4, and the bagels come in packs of 6. What is the least number of muffins and bagels you need to have the same number of each? How many packs of each food do you need?

_____

6.NS.5 Understand that positive and negative numbers are used together to describe quantities having opposite directions or values (e.g., temperature above/below zero, elevation above/below sea level, credits/debits, positive/negative electric charge); use positive and negative numbers to represent quantities in real-world contexts, explaining the meaning of 0 in each situation.

Real World Connections

Key Words

positive numbers

negative numbers

When the temperature drops below freezing, exposed water pipes and plants outside should be protected. You need a way to express the temperature in relation to the freezing point of water. Whether a value is above or below a given point can be described using positive and negative numbers. Any quantities that have opposite values or directions can be described in this way.

Positive numbers are numbers that are greater than zero. A positive number is used to represent an increase in a quantity, such as +$15 extra in the bank from shoveling snow or having +5 inches of snow on the ground after a storm. Positive numbers are also used to represent an amount above a certain level, such as having a balance of +$50 in your savings account or being above sea level at an elevation of +200 feet.

Negative numbers are numbers that are less than zero. A negative number is used to represent a decrease in a quantity, such as −$10 on the cost of an item that is on sale. Negative numbers are also used to represent an amount below a certain level, such as lake levels being at −10 feet after a drought or being below sea level at an elevation of −150 feet.

Positive and negative numbers can also be used to represent direction. Objects that move in opposite directions (up versus down or right versus left) can be described using positive and negative numbers.

The meaning of a positive number or of a negative number depends on what 0 means in that situation. When discussing elevation, 0 represents sea level. When discussing electric charge, 0 represents having no charge.

 Peoples Common Core Mathematics

Take It Apart

To use and understand positive and negative numbers, follow some simple steps.

Step 1   Analyze what 0 means in the situation.

Temperature is often described in relation to the freezing point of water. On the Celsius scale, the freezing point of water is 0°C.

Step 2   Determine whether your value is above or below the value of 0.

On the thermometer, the temperature shown is below 0°C.

Step 3   Determine if you should represent the value using a positive number or a negative number. Your choice should reflect what you determined in Step 2.

The temperature reading is below zero, so you should represent it using a negative number. The temperature is −5°C, which is 5 degrees Celsius below freezing. You'll need to protect the pipes and plants!

Write a number to represent each situation.

1. a temperature of 15 degrees below zero

2. at the freezing point

_____

_____

3. the temperature rose 10 degrees

4. the temperature dropped 20 degrees

_____

_____

Put It Together

Use what you now know about positive and negative numbers to write a number to represent each situation.

1. an elevation 430 feet above sea level

   _____

2. a temperature of 10 degrees below zero

   _____

3. an increase of 2 points on your average

   _____

4. a withdrawal of $120 from a savings account

   _____

5. a height 2 inches below the average

   _____

6. a golf score of 3 strokes over par

   _____

Answer the questions. Share your ideas with a classmate.

7. Atoms are composed of protons, neutrons, and electrons. A proton has a positive charge, a neutron has no charge, and an electron has a negative charge. How can these charges be represented using positive and negative numbers?

   _____

8. A cat climbs 10 feet up a telephone pole and then slides down 4 feet. Represent each distance using positive and negative numbers. What does the number 0 represent in this example?

   _____

   _____

Make It Work

Answer the questions below.

1. Which number would represent a location that is thirty feet above sea level?

   A. −13

   B. +13

   C. −30

   D. +30

2. Which number would represent a temperature of "fourteen below"?

   A. −14

   B. −40

   C. +14

   D. +40

3. In football, the gain or loss of yards is described as being "from the line of scrimmage." What number is the line of scrimmage associated with in these descriptions?

   _____

4. Describe a situation in which you would like a +$10 change and a situation in which you would not like a +$10 change. Explain your answer.

   _____

   _____

   _____

5. Two birds start flying from the same branch at the same time. They fly for the same amount of time. Each bird travels at a rate of 20 miles per hour. But, the birds end up miles apart. How can this puzzle be explained using positive and negative numbers?

   _____

   _____

   _____

Lesson 17 Identifying Opposites on a Number Line

6.NS.6.a Recognize opposite signs of numbers as indicating locations on opposite sides of 0 on the number line; recognize that the opposite of the opposite of a number is the number itself, e.g., $-(-3) = 3$, and that 0 is its own opposite.

Real World Connections

Key Word

opposite

numbers

To determine partners for a math project, your teacher has the students form a line. Your teacher then steps right in the middle of the line so that half of the students are on her left and half are on her right. She says that the class is now a number line and that each person will be the partner of his or her opposite.

Opposite numbers are two numbers that are the same distance from zero on a number line, but in different directions. For example, $+5$ and -5 are opposite numbers. The opposite signs of the numbers indicate that the numbers are located on opposite sides of zero. Each number is 5 units away from zero on a number line, but $+5$ is five units to the right of zero and -5 is five units to the left of zero.

The number *0* is the number that divides the number line. It is the point from which distances on the number line are measured. As a result, zero is its own opposite. So, the opposite of 0 is 0.

An opposite of a number is the same distance from zero but on the opposite side of zero from the original number. If you take the opposite of the opposite of a number, you will move from one side of zero to the other and back again. As a result, you will end up back at the original number. For example, the opposite of $+5$ is -5. And the opposite of -5 is $+5$. So, the opposite of the opposite of $+5$ is $+5$.

         Peoples Common Core Mathematics

Take It Apart

To identify opposite numbers, follow some simple steps.

Step 1 Draw a number line.

Imagine that the number line below shows the names of some of your classmates and their positions in the number line.

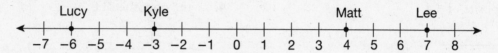

Step 2 Graph your number on the line.

Imagine that you are at +3. Graph your position on the line.

Step 3 Find the number that is the same distance from zero as your number is, but on the opposite side of zero.

Your number is three places to the right of zero, so the opposite number is three places to the left of zero. The opposite of +3 is −3, so you would be working with Kyle on this project.

Because the sign of a number indicates which side of zero the number is on, if you change the sign of a number you find that number's opposite.

Use the strategy and number line above to answer the following questions about opposites.

1. What is the opposite number for Lee's position?

_____

2. If you wanted to work with Lucy, how should you change your position?

_____

3. What is the opposite number for Matt's position?

_____

Put It Together

Use what you now know about opposites to find each number.

1. the opposite of +12

    _____

2. the opposite of −5

    _____

3. the opposite of +4

    _____

4. the opposite of 0

    _____

5. −(−(−8))

    _____

6. the opposite of the opposite of the opposite of +10

    _____

Answer the questions. Share your ideas with a classmate.

7. Why is zero its own opposite?

    _____

    _____

    _____

8. Describe a rule that states how many spaces to the left you would have to move from any positive number to reach its opposite.

    _____

    _____

    _____

Make It Work

Answer the questions below.

1. Which of the following is the opposite of the opposite of negative ninety?

A. -90

B. -19

C. $+19$

D. $+90$

2. Which pair of numbers are opposites?

A. -8 and $-(-8)$

B. $+5$ and $-(-5)$

C. $+7$ and 7

D. -4 and $-(-(-4))$

3. Which points represent opposites?

_____

4. The number -10 is farther to the left than the number -4 is on a number line. How do the locations of their opposites compare?

_____

_____

5. Determine a rule for whether your answer will have the opposite sign or the same sign as the starting number based on the number of times you take the opposite.

_____

_____

_____

Lesson 18 Using Signs to Identify the Quadrant of an Ordered Pair

6.NS.6.b Understand signs of numbers in ordered pairs as indicating locations in quadrants of the coordinate plane; recognize that when two ordered pairs differ only by signs, the locations of the points are related by reflections across one or both axes.

Real World Connections

Key Words

coordinate
  plane

x-axis

y-axis

origin

ordered pair

x-coordinate

y-coordinate

quadrants

While playing a game, you have sunk all of your friend's ships but one. You look at the grid. You see the pegs that mark each of your earlier shots. You see a likely target and call out the coordinates, "B-5!" Your friend lets out a groan and says, "Hit and sunk!" You've won!

The key to the game described is to use coordinates to identify points on a plane. A **coordinate plane** is a system used to locate points represented along horizontal and vertical axes. The **x-axis** is the horizontal number line in the coordinate plane. The **y-axis** is the vertical number line in the coordinate plane. The **origin** is the point where the axes intersect. It is identified by the ordered pair (0, 0). An **ordered pair** is a pair of numbers used to identify a point in the coordinate plane. The **x-coordinate** is the first number in an ordered pair. It tells the direction and number of units to move horizontally. The **y-coordinate** is the second number in an ordered pair. It tells the direction and number of units to move vertically.

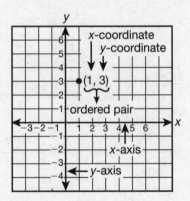

The axes divide the coordinate plane into four regions, or **quadrants**. Each quadrant is identified by a Roman numeral. You can tell which quadrant an ordered pair is in based on the signs of the numbers in the ordered pair.

 Peoples Common Core Mathematics

Take It Apart

To determine which quadrant a point is in, follow some simple steps.

Step 1 Find the *x*-coordinate of the ordered pair.

The *x*-coordinate of the ordered pair (3, 2) is +3. It represents moving 3 units to the right along the horizontal axis.

Step 2 Find the *y*-coordinate of the ordered pair.

The *y*-coordinate of the ordered pair (3, 2) is +2. It represents moving 2 units up along the vertical axis.

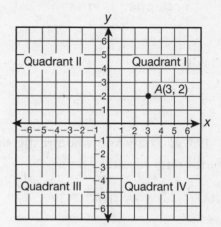

Step 3 Plot the point and identify the quadrant in which it is located.

The location of the point (3, 2) is in the upper-right quadrant. This region is Quadrant I.

If two ordered pairs differ only by the sign of one or both coordinates, then the locations of the points are related by reflections across one or both axes. For example, (−3, 2) is a point that is located 3 units to the left and 2 units up from the origin. This point is a reflection of the point at (3, 2) across the *y*-axis and is located in Quadrant II.

Use the strategy and coordinate plane above to answer the following questions.

1. In which quadrant is the point (−2, −4)?

   _____

2. What are the coordinates of the reflection of (3, 2) across the *x*-axis?

   _____

3. In which quadrant is the reflection of (3, 2) across the *x*-axis?

   _____

Put It Together

Use what you now know about ordered pairs to identify the quadrant in which each point is located.

1. $(-10, 15)$

2. $(7, -14)$

3. $(-3, -12)$

Use what you now know about the signs of the coordinates in ordered pairs to identify the resulting point.

4. $(31, -22)$ reflected across the x-axis

5. $(-13, -13)$ reflected across the y-axis

Answer the questions. Share your ideas with a classmate.

6. Describe a reflection across an axis in terms of opposite numbers.

7. What effect on the signs of the coordinates does a reflection across the y-axis have?

Make It Work

Answer the questions below.

1. Which of the following ordered pairs is located in Quadrant III?

   A. $(-4, 6)$ **B.** $(4, 6)$

   C. $(4, -6)$ **D.** $(-4, -6)$

2. Which of the following is the ordered pair for the reflection of $(-7, 3)$ across the x-axis?

   A. $(-7, -3)$ **B.** $(7, -3)$

   C. $(3, -7)$ **D.** $(-3, 7)$

3. Examine the coordinate plane shown. Identify the pairs of points that are reflections over a single axis.

   _____

   _____

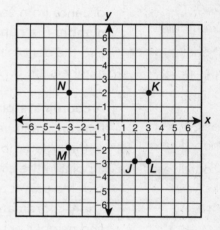

4. The coordinates in an ordered pair have opposite signs. What can you conclude about the quadrant in which the ordered pair is located? Explain your answer.

   _____

   _____

   _____

   _____

5. A point in Quadrant II is reflected over one axis and this new point is reflected over the other axis. What is the effect of reflecting over the x-axis followed by reflecting over the y-axis compared with the effect of reflecting over the y-axis followed by reflecting over the x-axis?

   _____

   _____

   _____

6.NS.6.c Find and position integers and other rational numbers on a horizontal or vertical number line diagram; find and position pairs of integers and other rational numbers on a coordinate plane.

Real World Connections

Toolbox

calculator

Key Words

integers

opposite
  numbers

rational number

coordinate
  plane

ordered pair

x-coordinate

y-coordinate

Whether you are trying to find a book on a library shelf or calculating how far your school is from your house using a map, locating points on a number line diagram or coordinate plane can help. How would you approach plotting $\frac{9}{4}$ and $-\frac{7}{4}$ on a number line diagram?

A number line diagram is a helpful tool for use in comparing integers and other rational numbers. **Integers** include all whole numbers and their opposites. You may remember that **opposite numbers** are two numbers that are the same distance from zero on a number line, but in different directions. A **rational number** is a number that can be written as a fraction, where the numerator and the denominator are integers and the denominator is not 0. Some rational numbers are 0.76, $3\frac{2}{3}$, -4, and $\frac{11}{21}$.

A **coordinate plane** is a system used to locate points represented along horizontal and vertical axes. Each axis is a number line, and the axes intersect at the ordered pair (0, 0). An **ordered pair** is a pair of numbers used to identify a point in the coordinate plane. The **x-coordinate** is the first number in an ordered pair. It tells the direction and number of units to move right or left. The **y-coordinate** is the second number in an ordered pair. It tells the direction and number of units to move up or down.

When plotting a point on a number line diagram or on a coordinate plane, you must know where the positive numbers and the negative numbers are located. The following table summarizes which way you should move from zero based on the sign of the number.

Orientation of number line (axis)	Positive number	Negative number
horizontal (x)	to the right	to the left
vertical (y)	up	down

Take It Apart

To plot a rational number on a number line diagram, follow some simple steps.

Step 1 Draw a number line diagram that covers the range of numbers you will need to plot. Rewrite any improper fraction as a mixed number to help locate it.

Rewriting the improper fraction $\frac{9}{4}$ as $2\frac{1}{4}$ and $-\frac{7}{4}$ as $-1\frac{3}{4}$ shows that a good range for your number line diagram is from -3 to $+3$.

Step 2 Determine which direction from 0 your number will be.

The positive number, $2\frac{1}{4}$, will be to the right of 0, and the negative number, $-1\frac{3}{4}$, will be to the left of 0.

Step 3 Draw divisions between the numbers that work well for the numbers that you need to plot.

Both numbers are in fourths, so marking off each fourth on the number line diagram is best.

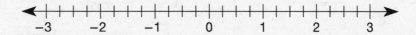

Step 4 Locate the number you need to plot and mark it on the number line diagram.

To plot a point on a coordinate plane, simply apply the above steps to each axis.

Use the strategy above to plot the following rational numbers on the number line diagram below.

1. -1 2. 0.6 3. $-\frac{4}{40}$

Put It Together

Use your tools and what you now know about rational numbers to identify the number represented by each point on the number line diagram.

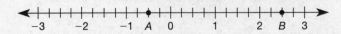

1. Point *A*

2. Point *B*

_____   _____

Use your tools and what you now know about rational numbers to identify the coordinates for each point on the coordinate plane.

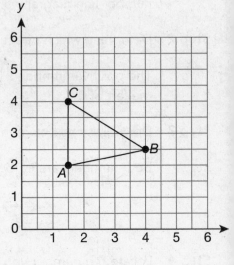

3. Point *A*   4. Point *B*   5. Point *C*

_____   _____   _____

Answer the questions. Share your ideas with a classmate.

6. Describe how you would help to teach a friend how to plot the point $(-3, 1.5)$ on a coordinate plane.

_____

_____

7. Describe when a number is a rational number. Why is there a limitation?

_____

_____

_____

Make It Work

Answer the questions below.

1. Which description for plotting (–5.4, 6.2) is correct?

A. move 5.4 units right

B. move 5.4 units down

C. move 6.2 units up

D. move 6.2 units right

2. Which point is located at –3?

A. Point *P*   **B.** Point *Q*

C. Point *R*   **D.** Point *S*

3. Plot and label the following points on the coordinate plane.

Point *X* (0, −1); Point *Y* (−$\frac{4}{2}$, 3.5), and Point *Z* (4.5, −1)

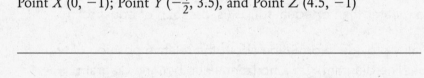

_____

_____

4. A point plotted on a coordinate plane is located on the *y*-axis. What can you conclude about the possible values of the *x*-coordinate? What can you conclude about the possible values of the *y*-coordinate? Explain your answer.

_____

_____

_____

5. A student plots 3 rational numbers on a single number line diagram but draws only a single point. One number is a decimal, one is a fraction with a denominator of 4, and one is a mixed number with a denominator of 2. Explain how this is possible and give a set of 3 rational numbers that demonstrate your answer.

_____

_____

_____

Lesson 20 Comparing and Ordering Numbers on a Line Diagram

6.NS.7.a Interpret statements of inequality as statements about the relative position of two numbers on a number line diagram. *For example, interpret −3 > −7 as a statement that −3 is located to the right of −7 on a number line oriented from left to right.*

Real World Connections

Key Word

inequality

You run into the grocery store to pick up a few cans of soup for a food drive at school. You remember how your math teacher was just describing how the aisles in the grocery store were arranged like a number line. You enter the store at aisle 8, and you know that soup is on aisle 4. Should you turn right or left?

Understanding how numbers compare and the order they appear on a number line diagram can help in situations like finding the right seat at a stadium, the right address on a street, and the right aisle to buy soup. To describe the positions of numbers on a number line, you must be able to interpret inequalities.

An **inequality** is a number sentence that states two expressions may not be equal. These symbols can be used to show an inequality: > (is greater than), < (is less than), ≥ (is greater than or equal to), ≤ (is less than or equal to).

Statements of inequality provide information about the relative position of two numbers on a number line diagram. On a horizontal number line diagram, numbers are shown from left to right in increasing order. So when you compare any two numbers on the number line, the number that is located farther left is always less than the number that is located farther right.

Another way to describe the relative positions on a number line diagram is to say that the number that is located farther right is always greater than the number that is located farther left.

Take It Apart

To decide the relative positions of numbers, follow some simple steps.

Step 1 Determine whether the inequality uses greater than or less than.

You know that 8 is greater than 4.

Step 2 The lesser number appears farther to the left on a number line diagram.

Because 4 is the lesser number, it is located farther to the left than 8 is.

Step 3 Plot the numbers on a number line diagram to check your answer.

On the number line diagram, 4 is clearly located to the left of 8. So, if you enter at aisle 8 you should turn left to find your soup.

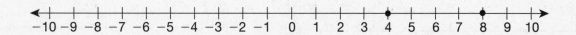

Keep in mind that there are two correct descriptions for the relative positions of the numbers in an inequality. In addition to saying that 4 is to the left of 8, you could also say that 8 is to the right of 4. Either statement is correct.

Use the strategy above to describe the relative locations of the numbers in each inequality.

1. $12 > 5$

_____

2. $0 < 6$

_____

3. $-11 < -10$

_____

Put It Together

Use what you now know about comparing and ordering numbers to describe the relative positions of the numbers in each inequality.

1. $9 > 4$

_____

2. $0 < 3$

_____

3. $-4 > -10$

_____

4. $-12 < -9$

_____

5. $0 > -1$

_____

6. $3 > -4$

_____

Answer the questions. Share your ideas with a classmate.

7. Write an analogy that describes the relationship between the terms greater than, to the left, to the right, and less than.

_____

_____

8. Write an inequality that supports the statement that all negative numbers are located to the left of 0.

_____

Make It Work

Answer the questions below.

1. Which statement correctly compares the numbers and describes their relative positions on a number line diagram?

   A. $8 > 12$; 8 is located to the left of 12

   B. $-5 > 1$; -5 is located to the right of 1

   C. $-4 < -2$; -4 is located to the left of -2

   D. $-1 < 2$; -1 is located to the right of 2

2. Given the inequality $-6 < 3$, which statement correctly describes the relative positions of 0, -6, and 3 on a number line diagram?

   A. -6 is located to the right of 0 and to the left of 3

   B. -6 is located to the left of 0 and to the left of 3

   C. -6 is located to the right of 0 and to the right of 3

   D. -6 is located to the left of 0 and to the right of 3

3. What can you tell about the relative positions of 6 and an unknown number x if you know that $6 > x$?

   _____

   _____

4. Yolanda says that -15 is greater than -5 because it is farther from 0 than -5 is. Analyze the accuracy of her statement and correct it if necessary.

   _____

   _____

   _____

5. You are asked to find a number that is greater than -3 and less than $+3$. Explain where you would find a number that matches the description. Is -10 a correct response? Explain your answer.

   _____

   _____

   _____

6.NS.7.b   Write, interpret, and explain statements of order for rational numbers in real-world contexts.
For example, write −3 °C > −7 °C to express the fact that −3 °C is warmer than −7 °C.

Real World Connections

The weather report states that the temperature will stay below −4 °C. Should you expect that the thermometer will show a reading of −2 °C?

It is important to understand the order of numbers in real-world situations. Knowing whether a number is greater than or less than another is useful when comparing prices, discounts, and temperatures. To write and explain statements of order of numbers you need to understand inequalities.

An **inequality** is a number sentence that states two expressions may not be equal. These symbols can be used to show an inequality: > (is greater than), < (is less than), ≥ (is greater than or equal to), ≤ (is less than or equal to).

Take It Apart

To write or interpret statements of order for numbers used in real-world situations, follow some simple steps.

Step 1 Identify what quantity the numbers are expressing.

The thermometer readings express temperatures.

Step 2 Consider the terms that are associated with comparing or ordering these quantities.

Temperatures are compared using terms such as *warmer* and *colder*.

Step 3 Write an inequality to show the comparison.

$-4\,°C < -2\,°C$

Step 4 Explain what the inequality says about the situation.

Because $-4\,°C$ is colder than $-2\,°C$, you should not expect the thermometer to show a temperature of $-2\,°C$.

Use the strategy above to answer the following questions about the order of numbers.

1. Write an inequality to express the fact that 2 °C is colder than 10 °C.

    _____

2. Write an inequality to express the fact that Miguel has $20 in his wallet, which is enough to buy the books he needs for $15.

    _____

3. Explain what is meant by the expression 4.2 feet < 4.6 feet when discussing the results of a long jump competition.

    _____

    _____

Put It Together

Use what you now know about ordering numbers to write an inequality to express the following numbers.

1. Rafiq was earning $7.55 per hour. He got a raise and is now earning $7.95 per hour.

   _____

2. A healthy puppy gets heavier during its first year. Spot was 7.4 pounds but has gotten heavier and is now 19.5 pounds.

   _____

3. A stock was valued at $2.30 per share, but its value dropped and is now only $1.75 per share.

   _____

Use what you now know about ordering numbers to interpret or explain each inequality.

4. $-4.5\,°C < 4.5\,°C$

   _____

5. 3.4 inches tall $<$ 6.4 inches tall

   _____

6. $399.99 $>$ $379.99

   _____

Answer the questions. Share your ideas with a classmate.

7. What are three real-life terms that can be used to interpret an inequality that uses the symbol $>$?

   _____

8. What symbol would you use if you were trying to express the fact that someone is no older than 13 years old? Explain your answer.

   _____

   _____

Make It Work

Answer the questions below.

1. Which symbol could you interpret as meaning "is lower in elevation than?"

   A. =

   B. >

   C. <

   D. ≥

2. Three friends, Mike, Jay, and Ramone, ran a 10-kilometer race. They compared their times to finish the race and saw that 43.5 minutes (Mike) < 45.6 minutes (Jay) < 51.4 minutes (Ramone). Which statement correctly interprets the results of the race?

   A. Mike took longer to finish than Jay did.

   B. Ramone took less time to finish than Mike did.

   C. Jay took less time to finish than Mike did.

   D. Ramone took longer to finish than Mike did.

3. Write an inequality to express the fact that the $20.00 gift card that you have is not enough to buy the $24.99 DVD that you wanted.

   _____

4. A news article exposes a store in which prices changed by +20%, −25%, and +10%. Write an inequality to show the order of the changes in prices.

   _____

5. Describe a time when you would use the symbol ≥. Write an inequality and interpret it to show how the symbol is used.

   _____

   _____

   _____

   _____

Lesson 22 Understanding and Interpreting Absolute Value

6.NS.7.c Understand the absolute value of a rational number as its distance from 0 on the number line; interpret absolute value as magnitude for a positive or negative quantity in a real-world situation. *For example, for an account balance of −30 dollars, write |−30| = 30 to describe the size of the debt in dollars.*

Real World Connections

Key Word

absolute value

You're trying to meet your friends at a sporting event, but you can't find them. You send a text message to one of your friends to tell her where you are. She replies to say that she's just 10 rows away. But which way should you go to find her: up or down?

Absolute values can help you to understand how to better express a distance in this situation. The **absolute value** of a number is the number's distance from zero on a number line. When you see a number in the symbol | |, you need to take the absolute value of the number. So $|-8|$ is read "the absolute value of negative eight."

To find the absolute value of a number, think about how far from zero the number appears on a number line. The number -8 is 8 units away from zero, so $|-8| = 8$. Likewise, the number $+8$ is 8 units away from zero, so $|+8| = 8$.

When expressing real-world situations, you can think of absolute value as the magnitude, or size, for a positive or negative quantity. Absolute value shows only the size of the amount and not whether the original amount was positive or negative. When using absolute value to express an actual amount, be sure to use descriptive words to avoid confusion.

 Peoples Common Core Mathematics

Take It Apart

To express real-world situations using absolute value, follow some simple steps.

Step 1   Determine the value of the amount you want to express.

In the example, consider the chance that your friend is 10 rows above where you are (+10 rows) and that she is 10 rows below where you are (−10 rows).

Step 2   Find the absolute value.

$|+10| = 10$ and $|−10| = 10$; notice that the absolute value is the same for each quantity.

Step 3   Use descriptive words that help to identify the real situation.

The words *up* and *down* work well in this situation because the positive and negative signs describe the direction from where you are.

Step 4   Express the quantities.

Describing her location as either 10 rows up or 10 rows down from where you are would have avoided any confusion.

Use the strategy above to answer the following questions that involve absolute value.

1. What is the absolute value of 6.4?

    _____

2. Evaluate $|−1.34|$.

    _____

3. A diver is at an elevation of −30 m. Use absolute value to express the location of the diver.

    _____

Put It Together

Use what you now know about absolute value to solve each of the following.

1. $|-7|$

    _____

2. $|4.3|$

    _____

3. $\left|-\frac{4}{7}\right|$

    _____

Use what you now know about absolute value to express each of the following.

4. The elevation of a kite is $+150$ feet.

    _____

5. The temperature is $-5\,°C$.

    _____

Answer the questions. Share your ideas with a classmate.

6. What can the absolute value of a number never be?

    _____

7. Why is it important to describe the meaning of an absolute value in a real-world situation using words such as *above* and *below*?

    _____

    _____

Make It Work

Answer the questions below.

1. Which statement best describes a person who has a bank account balance of –55 dollars?

   A. The person has $|-55 \text{ dollars}| = 55$ dollars in the bank.

   B. The person has $|-55 \text{ dollars}| = -55$ dollars in the bank.

   C. The person is $|-55 \text{ dollars}| = 55$ dollars in debt.

   D. The person is $|-55 \text{ dollars}| = -55$ dollars in debt.

2. How do the absolute values of a number and its opposite compare?

   A. They are never the same.

   B. They are always the same.

   C. The absolute value of the positive number is always greater.

   D. The absolute value of the negative number is always greater.

3. If you know how far a number is from zero on a number line, do you also need to know whether the number is to the right or left of zero to write its absolute value? Explain your answer.

_____

_____

_____

4. What can you conclude about the position of a number on a number line if you know the absolute value of the number? What can you not determine about the location of the number? Explain your answer using the term magnitude.

_____

_____

_____

5. A canyon floor is at an elevation of -500 m as viewed from the edge of the canyon. A hawk is flying 400 m above the canyon floor. An eagle is flying 600 m above the canyon floor. Use absolute value to express the location of the canyon floor, the location of the hawk, and the location of the eagle as viewed from the edge of the canyon.

_____

_____

_____

Lesson 23 Comparing Absolute Value and Order

6.NS.7.d Distinguish comparisons of absolute value from statements about order. *For example, recognize that an account balance less than −30 dollars represents a debt greater than 30 dollars.*

Real World Connections

Key Word

absolute value

The balance on your library account is −$1.50 because of an overdue book. The balance on your cafeteria account is −$2.25. How do the balances compare? At which location do you have the larger debt?

Answering these questions requires an understanding of absolute value. The **absolute value** of a number is the number's distance from zero on a number line. The symbol │ │ is used when you need to take the absolute value of a number.

When expressing real-world situations, you can think of absolute value as the magnitude, or size, for a positive or negative quantity. Absolute value shows only the size of the amount and not whether the original amount was positive or negative. When using absolute value to express an actual amount, be sure to use descriptive words to avoid confusion.

Often, there is one word for the actual quantity and a different word when comparing absolute values. For example, the balance in an account can be positive or negative, but the debt that someone owes is the absolute value of a negative account balance.

For negative numbers, the absolute value gets larger as the actual value gets smaller. As a result, you must be careful when you compare absolute values and when you describe the order of numbers. Just because one number is less than another does not mean its absolute value will be less. And if you are comparing the absolute values of real-world amounts, keep in mind that the comparison does not immediately provide information about the order of the quantities.

                               Peoples Common Core Mathematics

Take It Apart

To compare and order numbers using absolute value, follow some simple steps.

Step 1 Decide whether you are looking at the actual quantity or at the absolute value based on the terms used.

The account balances describe the actual quantity, as they can have positive or negative values. The debt that you owe is a positive number and is an absolute value of a negative account balance.

Step 2 Compare the values for one of the terms used.

Compare the balances.

Library balance: −$1.50   Cafeteria balance: −$2.25

−$1.50 > −$2.25

Step 3 Compare the values for the other term used.

Compare the debts. The debts are the absolute values of the account balances.

Library debt: $|-\$1.50| = \$1.50$.   Cafeteria debt: $|-\$2.25| = \$2.25$

$1.50 < $2.25

Step 4 Describe your findings. Choose your terms carefully.

The balance on the library account is greater than the balance on the cafeteria account. The debt at the library is less than the debt at the cafeteria.

Use the strategy above to answer the following questions that involve comparing absolute values and quantities.

1. Compare the elevation and the depth of a fish swimming at −10 m with a clam resting at −50 m.

   _____

2. Compare the elevation and the altitude of a bird flying at 200 feet with an airplane flying at 5,000 feet.

   _____

   _____

Put It Together

Use what you now know about absolute value to circle the correct term in each pair to make a true statement.

1. To be farther below zero than −10 °C, the temperature must be (less than, greater than) −10 °C because the absolute value of the temperature will be (less than, greater than) 10.

2. When a bank account balance is less than −$200, the debt is (less than, greater than) $200 because the absolute value of the balance is (less than, greater than) 200.

3. A diver at −20 m in the ocean begins to slowly return to the surface. When the diver is halfway to the surface, her (elevation, depth) is greater than it was. The absolute value of her new elevation is (less than, greater than) 20.

Answer the questions. Share your ideas with a classmate.

4. When will a lesser number also have a lesser absolute value?

_____

5. How can one number be less than another and the absolute values of the numbers be the same? Give an example to support your answer.

_____

_____

Make It Work

Answer the questions below.

1. Which of the following bank account balances represents a debt that is greater than $50?

   A. −$75   **B.** −$50

   C. −$25   **D.** $25

2. A whale is swimming at an elevation of −200 feet. The depth of a shark swimming nearby is less than the depth of the whale. Which of the following elevations might be the shark's?

   A. −300 feet   **B.** −200 feet

   C. −100 feet   **D.** 100 feet

3. Circle the correct term in each pair to make a true statement.

   As you pay off a debt, the balance in the account (increases, decreases) and the debt (increases, decreases).

4. During a game show, the absolute value of a contestant's score is 30 points after the second round. After the third round, the absolute value of the score is 45 points. Explain why it is possible that the contestant has a lower score after the third round than after the second round.

   _____

   _____

   _____

5. In golf, the lowest score wins. During a given round, the winner shot a score of 65. Compare the winner's score with the scores of the other players. The winner shot −4 for the round. The runner-up was only 2 shots away from the winner. What did the runner-up shoot for the round? Explain your answer.

   _____

   _____

   _____

   _____

Solving Problems Involving Graphing Points on a Coordinate Plane

6.NS.8 Solve real-world and mathematical problems by graphing points in all four quadrants of the coordinate plane. Include use of coordinates and absolute value to find distances between points with the same first coordinate or the same second coordinate.

Real World Connections

Key Words

coordinate
plane
ordered pair
x-coordinate
y-coordinate

You are heading to a friend's house just down the street to work on a project. How can you figure out how far away the house is?

Knowing how to plot points on a coordinate plane and how to calculate absolute value can help you solve and find the distance between two points. A **coordinate plane** is a system used to locate points represented along horizontal and vertical axes. Each axis is a number line, and the axes intersect at the ordered pair (0, 0). An **ordered pair** is a pair of numbers used to identify a point in the coordinate plane. The **x-coordinate** is the first number in an ordered pair. It tells the direction and number of units to move right or left. The **y-coordinate** is the second number in an ordered pair. It tells the direction and number of units to move up or down.

To find the distance between points that have the same first coordinate or the same second coordinate you need to calculate the difference between the values of the unlike coordinate. The distance between the points is the absolute value of this difference.

Take It Apart

To determine the distance between two points that have one coordinate that is the same, follow some simple steps.

Step 1 Determine the coordinates of the points.

The streets in your neighborhood are arranged like a coordinate plane, and each block is 500 feet. Your friend's house is located at point *K* and your house is located at point *N*. So, the coordinates of the two points are (3, 2) and (−3, 2).

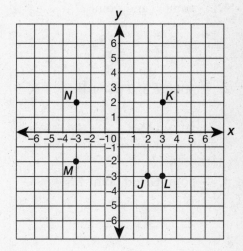

Step 2 Subtract the coordinates that are not the same.

The *x*-coordinates are not the same. −3 −3 = −6

Step 3 Find the absolute value of this difference.

$|-6| = 6$; your friend's house is 6 blocks away.
If each block is 500 feet long, then you have to travel
6 × 500 feet = 3,000 feet to get to your friend's house.

What if you switched the order of the numbers when you subtract them?
Then, 3 − (−3) = 3 + 3 = 6, and $|6| = 6$. The distance between the points is the same.

Use the above strategy to find the distance between the following points.

1. point *M* and point *N*

_____

2. point *K* and point *L*

_____

3. point *J* and point *L*

_____

  **Put It Together**

Use what you now know to find the distance between the points.

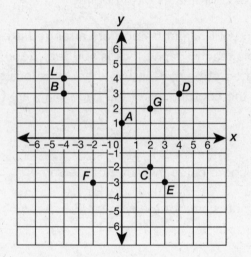

1.   point *B* and point *D*

   _____

2.   point *F* and point *E*

   _____

3.   point *G* and point *C*

   _____

Use what you now know about distance between points to determine the coordinates of the following points.

4.   a point that is in Quadrant II and is 5 units away from point *A*

   _____

5.   two points that are in Quadrant III and that are 4 units away from point *F*

   _____

Answer the questions. Share your ideas with a classmate.

6.   Where is a point located if it has the same *x*-coordinate as the origin?

   _____

7.   Which point is farther from (3, 5): (3, 10) or (−4, 5)? Explain your answer.

   _____

   _____

Make It Work

Answer the questions below.

1. What is the distance between $(4, -3)$ and $(-3, -3)$?

    A. -7

    B. 0

    C. 6

    D. 7

2. What is the distance between $(-2, -5)$ and its reflection over the *x*-axis?

    A. -10

    B. -4

    C. 4

    D. 10

Jamie and Melinda made a map of their town on a coordinate plane where each line represents 1 mile. Use the map to answer questions 3 and 4.

3. There is a park located north of Jamie's house where her street and Melinda's street meet. What are the coordinates of the park?

    _____

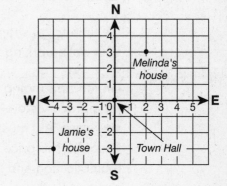

4. Each girl leaves her home and meets the other girl at the park. Compare the distance that each girl travels. Show your work.

    _____

    _____

    _____

5. A student wants to find the distance between two points by simply subtracting the unlike coordinates. When will this process give the correct answer?

    _____

    _____

    _____

Kick It Up!

Question 1: Can you figure out the fractions?

Using fraction bars to solve a problem that involves fractions is a helpful tool. And being able to work backwards by analyzing a set of fraction bars to determine the original problem is a great skill to practice to better understand this tool.

Make a question that involves dividing a whole number by a fraction and a second question that involves dividing a fraction by a fraction. Draw the solution to each problem using fraction bars. Exchange fraction bars with another student. Based on the model, write out the division problem that it was made to answer.

Question 2: How are decimals important while shopping?

It's time to go shopping! Calculations with money are a great way to practice your skills working with decimals.

Create a shopping list of at least 10 different items. Your list could involve food (at a grocery store or a restaurant), clothing, electronics, or anything else that you want. You must plan to purchase 2–4 pieces of at least 3 items on your list. Research the price of each item. Write a receipt for your purchase that shows the multiplication and addition needed to determine the total cost. Then, find out your share of the cost if you were to split it among 4 people.

Question 3: How many of each do you need?

The fact that a package of hot dogs and a package of hot dog buns have different numbers of items is often used in teaching least common multiple.

Think of two pairs of items. Like hot dogs and hot dog buns, the items within each pair must naturally go together and must come in packages that contain different numbers of items. Determine the number of packages of each item you would need so that you would have no items left over. Illustrate your findings on a poster to show how the numbers of items match up.

Chapter 2

Question 4: How far does school take you?

Locate a map of your school that is drawn to scale. Using the scale on the map, draw a coordinate plane on the map with the origin in roughly the center of the school. (Orient the grid of the coordinate plane so that the axes and the hallways run parallel as much as possible.)

Think through the places that you visit in the school on a typical day. Plot points at each room and hallway intersection along the path that you travel so that you move only horizontally or vertically from point to point. Mark each point with its coordinates to the nearest tenth of a unit on your map.

Write out a brief description of each leg of your trip. Next to each description, identify the points that you pass that are marked on the map. Using these points, calculate the distance that you travel. Be sure to show your work.

Add the distances to determine how far you travel in school in a typical day. Compare your total with your classmates'.

Lesson 25 Writing and Evaluating Numerical Expressions

6.EE.1   Write and evaluate numerical expressions involving whole-number exponents.

Real World Connections

Tracy and her family are planning to make an unusual patio in their large backyard. They are using square blocks to form a series of square regions, starting with a side of 1, then a side of 2, then a side of 3, and so on. One of Tracy's tasks is to calculate the number of square blocks they will need for the patio. Tracy figured out that the number of square blocks she needs is

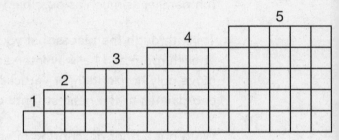

$$1^2 + 2^2 + 3^2 + 4^2 + 5^2 = 1 + 4 + 9 + 16 + 25 = 55$$

A **numerical expression** is any group of numbers, symbols, or letters that represents a quantity. Some examples of numerical expressions are 5, $5 + 17$, and $3^2 - \frac{3}{4}$.

In the expression 4^2, the number 2 is called an **exponent** and the number 4 is called a **base**.

4^2

base   exponent

An exponent tells you how many times a base appears as a factor.
For example, the expression 8^4 has base 8 and exponent 4. So 8^4 represents the product $8 \cdot 8 \cdot 8 \cdot 8$, which is 4,096.

Take It Apart

Follow these steps to find the number of square blocks needed for this patio.

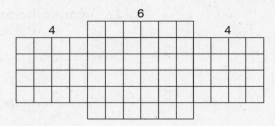

Step 1 Write an expression using exponents.

Step 2 Evaluate each part of the expression.

Step 3 Simplify the expression.

$4^2 + 6^2 + 4^2$

$16 + 36 + 16$

68

You need 68 square blocks to make the patio shown in the diagram.

Use the strategy above to solve these problems. Use a calculator and show your work.

1. Find the number of square blocks needed for this patio.

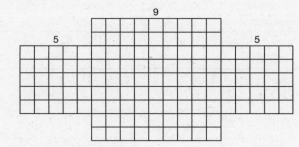

_____

_____

_____

2. The faces of a cube are squares. The volume of a cube with an edge of 4 units is shown using 4^3.

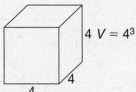

4 $V = 4^3$

3. Follow the steps above to find the volume of the figure below, which is formed by 3 cubes.

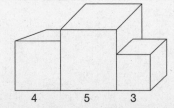

_____

_____

Put It Together

Now use what you know about expressions and exponents to solve these problems.

1. Write an expression using an exponent to represent the area of a square with a side length of 13 inches.

_____

2. Evaluate the expression $3^2 \cdot 2^5$.

_____

3. The volume of a cube is represented by the expression 9^3. Find the volume of the cube.

_____

4. Write an expression for the phrase "three squared plus seven cubed."

_____

Answer the questions. Talk about your answers with the class.

5. Explain what 17^2 can represent and explain what 17^3 can represent.

_____

_____

_____

6. Explain the difference between evaluating 5^6 and 6^5.

_____

_____

7. Suppose $x = 8$ and $y = 3$. Explain how you would evaluate x^y and how you would evaluate y^x.

_____

_____

_____

Make It Work

Answer the questions below.

1. For the expression 5^4, which statement is correct?

    A. 4 is the base.

    B. 4 is the exponent.

    C. 5 is the exponent.

    D. $5^4 = 4 \cdot 4 \cdot 4 \cdot 4$

2. Which of the expressions below has the greatest value?

    A. 6^2 **B.** 5^3

    C. 5^2 **D.** 3^2

3. The volume of a cube with edge length n is n^3. Use that pattern to write an expression for the volume of a cube with edge length $(a + 2b)$. Label the base and label the exponent for your expression.

4. A playground has four square-shaped sections for climbing and swinging equipment. The lengths of the sides of the four sections are 12 feet, 12 feet, 21 feet, and 25 feet. Write an expression using exponents to represent the total area of the four sections. Then evaluate your expression.

5. A small cube with side length x fits inside a larger cube with side length y. Use exponents to represent the volumes of the two cubes. Then write an expression that represents the difference between the two volumes. Finally, find the difference of the volumes if the side length of the smaller cube is 6 centimeters and the side length of the larger cube is 8 centimeters.

6.EE.2.a Write expressions that record operations with numbers and with letters standing for numbers. *For example, express the calculation "Subtract y from 5" as 5 − y.*

Real World Connections

The Sixth Grade Fair Committee is planning to decorate the school gym with crepe paper, posters, and tablecloths. They know that crepe paper costs $3 per roll, posters cost $12 each, and tablecloths cost $10 per table.

The committee used the expression $3r + 12p + 10t$ to represent the cost of r rolls of crepe paper, p posters, and t tablecloths. So the cost for 10 rolls of crepe paper, 5 posters, and 15 tablecloths would be

$3(10) + 12(5) + 10(15)$ or $30 + 60 + 150 = \$240$

A **variable** is a letter that is used to represent a number.

A **variable expression** is any group of numbers, variables, operation symbols, and grouping symbols.

The math processes of addition, subtraction, multiplication, and division are called **operations**.

When a number is multiplied by a variable, such as $10 \times t$ or $10 \cdot t$, that product can be written as "$10t$".

Take It Apart

Follow these steps to find how much money the committee needs for 8 rolls of crepe paper, 15 posters, and 13 tablecloths.

Step 1 Write the variable expression that the committee can use.

Step 2 Substitute the values $r = 8$, $p = 15$, and $t = 13$.

Step 3 Evaluate the expression.

$3r + 12p + 10t$
$3(8) + 12(15) + 10(13)$
$24 + 180 + 130 = \$334$

The decorations would cost \$334.

Here is another example. Suppose the committee has a budget of \$250. Use a strategy like the one above to see how much money will be left over if they use 5 rolls of crepe paper, 8 posters, and 13 tablecloths.

Step 1 Write the variable expression that shows the costs subtracted from \$250.

Step 2 Substitute the values $r = 5$, $p = 8$, and $t = 13$.

Step 3 Evaluate the expression.

$250 - (3r + 12p + 10t)$
$250 - (3 \cdot 5 + 12 \cdot 8 + 10 \cdot 13)$
$250 - (15 + 96 + 130)$
$250 - (241) = 9$

The committee would have \$9 left over.

Use the strategy above to solve these problems. Show your work.

1. Write a variable expression for the calculation "two times a variable, x plus fifteen times a variable, y."

2. Evaluate the variable expression $5a - 3b^2$ if $a = 10$ and $b = 2$.

3. Write a variable expression for eight times a variable, d, minus three times a variable, e, minus a variable, f. Then evaluate your expression for $d = 12$, $e = 5$, and $f = 11$.

Put It Together

Evaluate each expression if $a = 7$, $b = 10$, and $c = 3$.

1. $5a - 4c$

2. $(a + 2b) \cdot (3 + 5c)$

3. Write a variable expression for the cost of g pads of graph paper at $2 per pad, p boxes of pencils at $3 per box, r rulers at $1 per ruler, and t rolls of tape at $2 per roll.

4. Evaluate your expression from question 3 if $g = 10$, $p = 5$, $r = 25$, and $t = 4$.

Answer the questions. Share your ideas with a classmate.

5. Here is a variable expression: $25 - (2a + 3b) + 4x$. Identify one or more examples in that expression for each of the following:

a variable   addition

subtraction   multiplication

6. One student says that the value of the variable expression $3x - 2y$ can be 13, while another student says the value of the expression can be 20. Find different values for the variables to show that each student is correct.

_____

_____

7. Your friend Robin is the equipment manager for a sports team. Explain how Robin could use variable expressions to keep records of equipment and uniforms.

_____

_____

_____

                     Peoples Common Core Mathematics

Make It Work

Answer the questions below.

1. Which expression represents seven times the variable *r* minus 5 times the variable *s*?

   A. $5r - 7s$

   B. $7r - 5s$

   C. $7r + 5s$

   D. $7s - 5r$

2. What is the value of the variable expression $18 - (4x + 3y)$ if $x = 2$ and $y = 3$?

   A. 1

   B. 6

   C. 17

   D. 19

3. Write a variable expression to represent the number of people who can travel in 10 busses and 15 vans. Use the variables *b* and *v*, and start by explaining what each variable represents.

   _____

   _____

4. Refer to the Fair Committee at the beginning of this lesson. Suppose the committee can spend up to $200 and they want to buy at least 8 rolls of crepe paper, 6 posters, and 5 tablecloths. How much money will they have after those purchases? Can they afford to buy 3 more posters and 2 more tablecloths? Explain.

   _____

   _____

   _____

5. At an after-school job, a student sells magazines for $3 each and sells newspapers for $2 each. Her weekly expenses are $25. Write a variable expression to represent her income for selling *m* magazines and *n* newspapers. If she sells 10 magazines and 12 newspapers during one week, how much money is left after she pays her weekly expenses?

   _____

   _____

   _____

Lesson 27 Identifying Parts of an Expression

6.EE.2.b Identify parts of an expression using mathematical terms (sum, term, product, factor, quotient, coefficient); view one or more parts of an expression as a single entity. *For example, describe the expression 2 (8 + 7) as a product of two factors; view (8 + 7) as both a single entity and a sum of two terms.*

Real World Connections

All the students in the sixth grade have the same teacher for math, Mr. Teller. Mr. Teller likes to tell stories about his part-time job at a pizza parlor when he was young. Many of the students realized that those stories were related to the day's math lesson.

One day Mr. Teller told a story about watching the cooks prepare pizzas. After stretching the dough, they created combinations — mushrooms and olives, sausages and pepperoni — and used different kinds of cheeses. The students were not surprised when that day's math lesson involved the "ingredients" that make up a numerical expression: things like sums, products, and factors.

A **numerical expression** combines numbers with operations and grouping symbols. Each part of an expression that is separated by "+" and/or "−" signs is a **term** of the expression. Examples of numerical expressions are 5 + 6, (7 + 8) × 9, and (10 × 12) − 2. In the first expression, 5 and 6 are terms; in the second expression, 7 and 8 are terms; and in the third expression, (10 × 12) and 2 are terms.

If an expression has two numbers combined using a multiplication symbol, that expression is a **product**. Some examples of products are 5 × 3 and 6 × 8 × 10. In a product, each number (or group of numbers) is a **factor**.

If an expression has two numbers combined using a plus sign, that expression is a **sum**. Some examples of a sum are 5 + 3 and 6 + 8 + 10.

If an expression has two numbers combined using a division sign, that expression is a **quotient**. Each of the symbols "÷", "/", and the fraction bar is a division symbol. Some examples of a quotient are 10 ÷ 4, $\frac{10}{4}$, and 10/4.

If a number is multiplied by another expression, the original number is a **coefficient**. Here are some examples that use 8 as a coefficient: 8 × (10 + 5), 8 × $\frac{5}{3}$, and (6 × 10) × 8.

Copying is illegal.   Peoples Common Core Mathematics

Take It Apart

Identify two sums, products, factors, quotients, and coefficients in this numerical expression:

$$8 \times \left(\frac{3+2}{5}\right) + 9 \times \left(\frac{4 \div 2}{2 \div 4}\right)$$

Step 1 A sum combines two numbers or expressions using a "+" sign. So "3 + 2" is one sum. The entire expression is also a sum.

Step 2 A product combines two numbers or expressions using a "×" sign. So $8 \times \left(\frac{3+2}{5}\right)$ and $9 \times \left(\frac{4 \div 2}{2 \div 4}\right)$ are two products. Each product contains two factors, so 8 and $\left(\frac{3+2}{5}\right)$ are factors of $8 \times \left(\frac{3+2}{5}\right)$.

Step 3 A quotient combines two numbers or an expression using a division sign. So two quotients in the expression are $\frac{3+2}{5}$ and $4 \div 2$.

Step 4 In the original expression, 8 is a coefficient for the value $8 \times \left(\frac{3+2}{5}\right)$ and 9 is a coefficient for the value $9 \times \left(\frac{4 \div 2}{2 \div 4}\right)$.

Use what you know about sums, products, factors, quotients, and coefficients to answer these questions.

1. Identify two sums and two products in this expression:

   10 + 11(12 + 13) − 15 × 16

   _____

   _____

2. Identify two quotients and two coefficients in this expression:

   $$\frac{16}{2(8+1)} - \frac{5(6 \div 2)}{5 \times 3}$$

   _____

   _____

3. Write a numerical expression that has a sum, a quotient, and a product as you read it from left to right. Then use the same numbers, in the same order, to write a numerical expression that has a product, a quotient, and a sum as you read it from left to right.

   _____

4. What is the value of the expression in Question 1? in Question 2? in the expression used at the top of this page?

   _____

Put It Together

Use what you know about the parts of a numerical expression to answer these questions.

1. Write an expression that uses 5×3 and $8 \div 2$ as terms.

_____

2. Tell whether the entire following expression is a sum, a product, or a quotient: $(6 - 2) \div (4 + 3)$.

_____

Answer the questions. Share your ideas with a classmate.

3. Refer to the original expression used at the top of the Take It Apart page. Besides $\frac{3 + 2}{5}$ and $4 \div 2$, what are two other quotients in the expression?

_____

4. Here is an analysis of the numerical expression $(4 + 2) \times (12 \div 6)$: As a single entity, it is a product, and the factors in that product are $4 + 2$ and $12 \div 6$. The factor $4 + 2$ is a sum, and the factor $12 \div 6$ is a quotient. Write an analysis of the numerical expression $(7 \times 8) + (5 \div 2)$.

_____

_____

_____

5. Write the numbers 2, 3, 4, 5 in that order, with space separating them. Then write operation symbols $(+, -, \times, \div)$ and parentheses around or between the numbers to produce an expression for each set of conditions.

a. The expression, as a whole, is a sum whose terms are sums.

_____

b. The expression, as a whole, is a product and 2 is a coefficient.

_____

c. The expression has three factors.

_____

Make It Work

Answer the questions below.

1. In the expression $3 - (5 \times (4 + 8))$, which part of the expression is a factor?

   A. 3

   B. 5

   C. 4

   D. $5 \times (4 + 8)$

2. In the expression $\frac{3 - 2}{5 \div 7} \times 8$, which of the following does not appear?

   A. a sum

   B. a product

   C. a quotient

   D. a coefficient

3. Explain what is meant by "as a single entity."

   _____

   _____

4. Insert parentheses and operation symbols before, between, or after the numbers 1, 1, 3, 2, in that order, so the value of your expression is as great as possible.

   _____

5. Explain how you can use the numbers 2, 3, and 4, in that order, to write an expression that has exactly one term. In your answer, explain what symbol(s) you must use, what symbols(s) you can use, and what symbol(s) you cannot use.

   _____

   _____

   _____

   _____

Lesson 28 — Evaluating Expressions at Specific Values of Variables

6.EE.2.c   Evaluate expressions at specific values of their variables. Include expressions that arise from formulas used in real-world problems. Perform arithmetic operations, including those involving whole-number exponents, in the conventional order when there are no parentheses to specify a particular order (Order of Operations). *For example, use the formulas $V = s^3$ and $A = 6s^2$ to find the volume and surface area of a cube with sides of length $s = \frac{1}{2}$.*

Real World Connections

Key Words

evaluate

multiplication
   operation

addition
   operation

parentheses

formula

conventional
   order of
   operations

Mr. Teller, the sixth grade math teacher, likes to tell stories about his part-time job at a pizza parlor. One story was about working at the cash register. When two people each ordered a pizza, at $6.50 each, and a soft drink, at $1.50 each, he knew that he had two different ways to calculate the total: 6.50 + 6.50 + 1.50 + 1.50 or 2(6.50 + 1.50). Mr. Teller also told about calculating the sales tax and total amount for each bill. The sales tax rate was 8% on food and beverages, so he could use two different formulas to find the total bill:

(1) Total Bill = (cost of meal) + 0.08(cost of meal) or
(2) Total Bill = 1.08 (cost of meal)

To **evaluate** (or simplify) the numerical expression 5 + 3 × 2, shown below, the first step is to perform the **multiplication operation** 3 × 2 to get 6. The second step is to perform the **addition operation** 5 + 6. The value of the original expression is 11.

First
operation   5 + 3 × 2   Second
                        operation
            (5 + 3) × 2

In the expression (5 + 3) × 2, shown above, the **parentheses** indicate that the first step is to find the sum 5 + 3, which is 8. Then the second step is to find the product 8 × 2. The value of the original expression is 16.

A **formula** is an equation, using variables, numbers, and operation symbols, which describes how to calculate one measurement based on values of other measurements. As examples: the formula $A = b \times h$ tells how to calculate the area A of a rectangle or parallelogram based on the lengths of the base, b, and height, h; the formula $V = s^3$ tells how to calculate the volume V of a cube based on the length, s, of a side of the cube.

The **conventional order of operations** tells what operations are performed before or after other operations. Examples are the two expressions at the left: 5 + 3 × 2 and (5 + 3) × 2. The first one has no parentheses, so the first operation is multiplication and the second is addition. In the second expression, the parentheses indicate that the first operation is addition and the second is multiplication.

Take It Apart

Example 1: Evaluate the expression

$1 + (2 + 3) \times (4 \div 2)$.

Step 1 Evaluate the two expressions inside sets of parentheses. $= 1 + 5 \times 2$

Step 2 Then perform the multiplication. $= 1 + 10$

Step 3 Finally, perform the addition. $= 11$

The value of $1 + (2 + 3) \times (4 \div 2)$ is 11.

Example 2: Use the formula $A = \frac{1}{2}h(b_1 + b_2)$ to find the area of a trapezoid with $h = 6$ centimeters, $b_1 = 10$ centimeters, and $b_2 = 16$ centimeters.

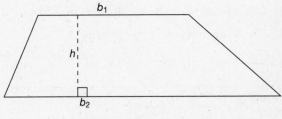

$$A = \frac{1}{2}h(b_1 + b_2)$$

Step 1 Write the formula. Substitute values for h, b_1, and b_2. $= \frac{1}{2}(6)(10 + 16)$

Step 2 Simplify the expression inside the parentheses. $= \frac{1}{2}(6)(26)$

Step 3 Perform the multiplications. $= 78$

The area of the trapezoid is 78 square centimeters.

Use what you know of the conventional order of operations to evaluate each numerical expression.

1. $15 + (7 - 3) \times (5 + 4)$

2. $\dfrac{(14 + 10) \div 2}{10 \div (3 + 2)} + 6$

_____

_____

3. A cashier at a restaurant has to find the total cost of food and beverages for three salads at $2.25 each, three sandwiches at $3.75 each, and three drinks at $1.10 each. Write three numerical expressions that can be used to find the total cost of food and beverages. Then evaluate any one of the numerical expressions.

_____

_____

_____

Put It Together

Evaluate each formula to find a measurement.

1. Use the formula $SA = 2(ab + bc + ac)$ to find the surface area SA of a rectangular prism if the dimensions of the prism are $a = 6\frac{1}{2}$ inches, $b = 8\frac{1}{2}$ inches, and $c = 2\frac{1}{4}$ inches.

   _____

2. Use the formula $V = Bh$ to find the volume V of a pentagonal prism if the area B of the base is $30\frac{1}{4}$ square centimeters and the height h of the prism is $10\frac{5}{8}$ centimeters.

   _____

Answer the questions. Share your ideas with a classmate.

3. The bill for food and beverages at a restaurant is $28.50. If the sales tax on food and beverages is 6%, then here are two expressions for the total bill:

   (1) Total Bill = (cost of meal) + 0.06(cost of meal)
   (2) Total Bill = 1.06(cost of meal)

   a. Substitute the given value for the "cost of meal" and show that both expressions give the same result.

   _____

   b. In expression (1), what does "0.06(cost of meal)" represent?

   _____

   c. In expression (1), the "cost of meal" at the end of the equation has a coefficient of 0.06. What is the coefficient of "cost of meal" that appears in the middle of the equation?

   _____

4. In a numerical expression, if there are no parentheses or grouping symbols then the conventional order of operations is to perform operations in parentheses first, then multiplication and division, then perform addition and subtraction. For each of the following numerical expressions, tell which operation you would do first and which operation you would do second. Then evaluate the numerical expression.

   a. $15\frac{1}{2} \times 10 + 8\frac{1}{2}$.

   _____

   b. $7\frac{1}{3} + 5\frac{2}{3} \times 3\frac{1}{2}$

   _____

Make It Work

Answer the questions below.

1. A formula for the area A of a triangle is $A = \frac{1}{2}bh$, where b and h are the base and height of the triangle. If the area of a triangle is 24 units², which choice represents possible values for b and h?

    A. $b = 6, h = 4$ **B.** $b = 8, h = 3$

    C. $b = 12, h = 6$ **D.** $b = 16, h = 3$

2. Which of the following numerical expressions has the least value?

    A. $2 \times 3 \times 4 + 5$ **B.** $(2 + 3 + 4) \times 5$

    C. $(2 \times 3) + (4 \times 5)$ **D.** $2 \times (3 + 4) \times 5$

3. In Example 2 on the Take It Apart page, one of the steps asks you to "substitute values." Explain what that means.

    _____

    _____

4. For a cube, find the value of the ratio $\frac{\text{surface area}}{\text{volume}}$ if the side of the cube is 4 units. What is the side of a cube for which that ratio is 1?

    _____

    _____

    _____

5. In the Real World Connection, Mr. Teller described two different ways to calculate a total. Write the two expressions. Then explain why they have the same value.

    _____

    _____

    _____

    _____

Lesson 29 Generating Equivalent Expressions

6.EE.3 Apply the properties of operations to generate equivalent expressions. *For example, apply the distributive property to the expression 3(2 + x) to produce the equivalent expression 6 + 3x; apply the distributive property to the expression 24x + 18y to produce the equivalent expression 6(4x + 3y); apply properties of operations to y + y + y to produce the equivalent expression 3y.*

Real World Connections

Key Words

variable

variable
    expression

equivalent

distributive
    property

Mr. Teller, the math teacher, reminded the students about a story from the previous lesson: If two people each ordered a pizza at $6.50 each and a drink at $1.50 each, then there were two ways to calculate the total: (6.50 + 1.50) + (6.50 + 1.50) or 2(6.50 + 1.50). Because the two numerical expressions have the same value, they are equivalent expressions.

Mr. Teller used that example to talk about equivalent expressions. It is easy to tell whether two numerical expressions are equivalent — simplify each of them, and if they have the same value then the expressions are equivalent. To decide whether two variable expressions are equivalent, there is an extra step. First, substitute numerical values for each variable. Second, test whether the resulting expressions are equivalent. If two variable expressions have the same value for any possible values of the variables, then the variable expressions must be equivalent.

A **variable** is a letter that represents a number. For example, in the expressions $3 + b$, $14 \times c$, (or $14c$), and $\frac{b + 2c}{3d}$, the letters b, c, and d are variables.

A **variable expression** is an expression that includes at least one variable and may also include numbers, operation symbols, and grouping symbols (such as parentheses). Each of the expressions $3 + b$, $14c$, and $\frac{b + 2c}{3d}$ is a variable expression.

Two expressions are **equivalent** if they have the same value. Examples: The numerical expressions 4×2 and $5 + 3$ are equivalent because each is equivalent to 8. The two variable expressions $5(a + 2b)$ and $5a + 10b$ are equivalent because for any values of a and b, the two expressions have the same value.

One way to generate equivalent expressions is to use the pattern $a(b + c) = ab + ac$, when any of the variables a, b, and c can be replaced with numbers. That pattern is called the **distributive property**. The distributive property can have several different forms:

$a(b + c) = ab + ac$ $a(b - c) = ab - ac$

$(b + c)a = ba + ca$ $(b - c)a = ba - ca$

Copying is illegal.   Peoples Common Core Mathematics

Take It Apart

Example 1: Use the distributive property to find an expression equivalent to $5(2a + 7)$. Then evaluate both expressions for $a = 3$ to confirm that the two expressions are equivalent.

Step 1 Use the distributive property pattern:
$x(y + z) = xy + xz$
$5(2a + 7) = 5 \times 2a + 5 \times 7$
$\qquad\quad = 10a + 35$

Step 2 Evaluate $5(2a + 7)$ and $10a + 35$ for $a = 3$:
$5(2a + 7) = 5(2 \times 3 + 7)$
$\qquad\quad\ = 5(6 + 7) = 5(13) = 65$
$10a + 35 = 10 \times 3 + 35 = 30 + 35 = 65$

Because $5(2a + 7)$ and $10a + 35$ have the same value, they are equivalent.

Example 2: Use the distributive property to find an expression equivalent to $3d + 5d$. Evaluate the two expressions for $d = 10$ to confirm that the two expressions are equivalent.

Step 1 One form of the distributive property is $ab + cb = (a + c)b$. Use that form to combine the terms:

$3d + 5d = (3 + 5)d$

Step 2 Simplify the coefficient of d:
$3d + 5d = (3 + 5)d = 8d$

Step 3 Evaluate $3d + 5d$ and $8d$ for $d = 10$:
$3d + 5d = 3 \times 10 + 5 \times 10 = 30 + 50 = 80$
$8d = 8 \times 10 = 80$

Because $3d + 5d$ and $8d$ have the same value, they are equivalent.

For each expression, use the distributive property to find an equivalent expression.

1. $12(2a + 5)$

_____

2. $-4(6x + 3y)$

_____

3. $(5a - b)(9)$

_____

4. $17\left(\dfrac{1}{x} + \dfrac{2}{y}\right)$

_____

5. $12g + 13g$

_____

6. $k + 2k + k$

_____

7. $15p + 30q$

_____

8. $20w + 30x + 50z$

_____

9. Use the distributive property to find an expression equivalent to $\dfrac{2a}{3b}(5a + 6)$. Be sure to reduce all the fractions in your answer.

_____

Put It Together

Use what you know about equivalent expressions to answer each question.

1. At a food court, 3 people spent x dollars each, 5 people spent y dollars each, and 4 more people spent x dollars each. Write a variable expression for the total amount that was spent. Then use properties of algebra to find an equivalent expression.

_____

Answer the questions. Share your ideas with a classmate.

2. The length of a rectangle is 15 inches and the width is $(x + 7)$ inches. Use the distributive property to write an expression, without using parentheses, for the number of square inches in the area of the rectangle.

_____

3. The area of a rectangle is $15p + 12$ square units. If the length of the rectangle is 3 units, what is the width? (*Hint*: Rewrite $15p + 12$ using the distributive property with 3 as the number outside the parentheses.)

_____

4. Solve Exercise 3 if the length of the rectangle is $\frac{1}{2}$ unit. Justify your answer.

_____

5. In the Real World Connection in the previous lesson, Mr. Teller told of using two different formulas to find the total bill if the sales tax rate on food and beverages was 6%. Find the two formulas that are mentioned for finding the total cost of the meal. Then explain how to use the distributive property to show that the two formulas for the total generate equivalent expressions. For variables, use T for the total bill and C for the cost of the meal.

_____

_____

_____

6. In algebra, terms such as $6a$ and $9a$ are called *like terms*. Another example of like terms are $12ab^2$, ab^2, and $-5ab^2$. They are called like terms because they can be combined:

    $6a + 9a = 15a$ $12ab^2 + ab^2 + (-5ab^2) = 8ab^2$

    What is needed for terms to be *like terms*?

_____

Make It Work

Answer the questions below.

1. Which expression is equivalent to $(5 + 3p)2$?

   A. $7 + 5p$ **B.** $10 + 5p$

   C. $10 + 6p$ **D.** $25 + 9p$

2. Which of the following expressions is not equivalent to the others?

   A. $2(12a + 18b)$ **B.** $3(8a + 9b)$

   C. $6(4a + 6b)$ **D.** $12(2a + 3b)$

3. Use the distributive property to find an expression equivalent to $6(2a - 5b)$. Then, using the values $a = 9$ and $b = 2$, explain how to show that the two variable expressions are equivalent.

   _____

   _____

   _____

4. Tell the coefficient of each term in the expression $p + 5p + p - 2p$. Then show how to use the distributive property to write a one-term expression that is equivalent to the given expression.

   _____

   _____

5. Write three expressions that are equivalent to $3x + 2$ that use only positive numbers and only the operations of multiplication and addition. Then write three more expressions that are equivalent to $3x + 2$ using the operations of multiplication, addition, and subtraction.

   _____

   _____

   _____

6. Explain how you can use properties of algebra, including the distributive property, to find this sum using mental math: $91 + 31 + 19 + 9 + 19 + 31 + 9 + 19 + 91 + 31$.

   _____

   _____

   _____

6.EE.4 Identify when two expressions are equivalent (i.e., when the two expressions name the same number regardless of which value is substituted into them). *For example, the expressions y + y + y and 3y are equivalent because they name the same number regardless of which number y stands for.*

Real World Connections

Key Words

variable
  expression
equivalent
equal sign
equation
inequality

During a class just before a holiday, Mr. Teller was describing how some ingredients were prepared before they would go into a pizza:

cheese: grated   mushrooms: sliced and spiced
sauce: stirred   sausage: sliced and sautéed

Mr. Teller pointed out that some ingredients (such as the cheese and sauce) had just one "operation" applied to them prior to use, while other ingredients (such as the mushrooms and sausages) had two "operations" applied to them prior to use.

The teacher used that story to introduce two kinds of variable expressions. One kind of expression has one operation performed on the variable:

$x + 4$ Add 4 to x. $z \div 0.5$ or $\frac{z}{0.5}$ Divide z by 0.5. $5y$ Multiply y by 5.

Mr. Teller said that some variable expressions (and the students would see many of these in later lessons) involve two operations:

$3x - 7$ Multiply the variable x by 3. Then subtract 7 from the result.
$\frac{y + 5}{2}$ Add 5 to the variable y. Then divide the result by 2.

A **variable expression** includes at least one variable and may also include numbers, operation symbols, and grouping symbols (such as parentheses). Examples: $3 + b$, $16z$, $15(3w - 12)$. Variable expressions are **equivalent** if they have the same value. Example: $5(a + 2b)$ and $5a + 10b$ have the same value for any values of a and b, so they are equivalent.

The "=" symbol is an **equal sign**. When an equal sign appears between two expressions, the result is an **equation**. The two sides of an equation are equivalent. Examples:
$2x = 10$ $2x$ and 10 have the same value.
$16 = x + 7$ 16 and $x + 7$ have the same value.

An **inequality**, like an equation, indicates a relationship between two expressions. Examples:

$2x < 10$ The value of $2x$ is less than 10.

$17 \leq y + 5$ The value 17 is less than or equal to the value of the expression $y + 5$.

$12 - z > 3$ The value of the expression 12 minus z is greater than 3.

$w + 15 \geq 0$ The value of the expression $w + 15$ is greater than or equal to the number 0.

 # Take It Apart

Example 1: Explain what operation is used to obtain the expression 7x. Then find the particular value of x that makes the expression 7x equivalent to the number 28. Finally, use equations to represent this problem and the particular value of x.

Step 1 To form the expression 7x, multiply the variable x by 7.

Step 2 If 7x and 28 are equivalent expressions, then x must be 4 because $7 \times 4 = 28$.

Step 3 One way to represent the situation that 7x and 28 are equivalent is to write the equation $7x = 28$. The particular value of x that makes 7x and 28 equivalent is the value 4, and one way to represent that particular value for x is to write the equation $x = 4$.

Example 2: Explain what operation is used to obtain the expression $z \div 4$. Then find several particular values of z that make $z \div 4$ greater than or equal to 1. Finally, use one inequality to represent this problem and another inequality to represent all the values of z.

Step 1 To form the expression $z \div 4$, divide the variable z by 4.

Step 2 If $z \div 4$ is greater than or equal to 1, then z can be 4 (because $4 \div 4 = 1$), or 5 (because $5 \div 4 > 1$) or 8 (because $8 \div 4 > 1$). In general, z can be any number greater than 4.

Step 3 The situation that $z \div 4$ is greater than or equal to 1 can be represented by the inequality $z \div 4 \geq 4$. The value of z can be any number greater than or equal to 1, and a way to represent all those values is the inequality $z \geq 4$.

1. Tell what operation is used to obtain the expression $x + 16$. Next, write an equation to represent the statement that $x + 16$ and 50 are equivalent. Finally, write an equation to represent the particular value of x that makes $x + 16$ equivalent to 50.

_____

2. Tell what operation is used to obtain the expression $w - 12$. Next, write an inequality to represent the statement that $w - 12$ is less than 9. Finally, write an inequality to represent the values of w that make $w - 12$ less than 9.

_____

3. A variable, d, is multiplied by 12, and the variable expression that results is equivalent to 60. Write that relationship as an equation. Then find the particular value of d that makes the variable expression equivalent to 60.

_____

Put It Together

Use what you know about equivalent expressions, equations, and inequalities to solve these problems.

1. On a pizza, 6 times the number of pepperoni slices, p, is equivalent to the number 30. Write an equation to represent that situation. Find the value of p that makes the two expressions equivalent, and write an equation to represent that value.

   _____

2. In a small restaurant, the number of customers, c, plus the 8 wait staff must be less than or equal to 45. Write an inequality to represent that situation. Find all the values for c that satisfy the inequality, and write another inequality to represent all those values of c.

   _____

Answer the questions. Share your ideas with a classmate.

3. Suppose the expression $3x + 4x + 2x$ is equivalent to the value 63. Use those two expressions to write an equation. Then write a second equation, for the same situation, that has one term on each side of the equal sign. Find the value of x that satisfies both of the equations, and write that value as a third equation.

   _____

4. Explain how an equation and an inequality are the same and how they are different.

   _____

   _____

   _____

   _____

   _____

   _____

   _____

Make It Work

Answer the questions below.

1. Which equation represents the situation that the variable expression $2x - 10$ is equivalent to the value 34?

    A. $2x = 10$ **B.** $2x - 10 = 34$

    C. $2x - 10 \leq 34$ **D.** $2x - 10 = 2x - 10$

2. All of the solutions to an inequality can be expressed using the inequality $x \geq 5$. What was the original inequality?

    A. $x + 17 > 5$ **B.** $x + 17 > 5$

    C. $x + 17 \geq 22$ **D.** $x - 5 \leq 0$

3. A variable t is multiplied by 5. The number 4 is subtracted from the product, and the resulting variable expression is equivalent to 6. Write an equation to represent the two equivalent expressions. Then write another equation to describe the value of t that makes the two expressions equivalent.

    _____

4. Suppose the solution to a problem is "$\frac{3x}{7} = 12$ or $\frac{3x}{7} < 12$." Write the solution as a single inequality.

    _____

5. A student is told that the expression $8x + 4x$ is equivalent to the number 48, and is also told that the expression $2y + 3y + y$ is equivalent to the expression $6y$. Represent each equivalence as an equation. Then explain how the two equations are different.

    _____

    _____

    _____

    _____

    _____

6.EE.5 Understand solving an equation or inequality as a process of answering a question: which values from a specified set, if any, make the equation or inequality true? Use substitution to determine whether a given number in a specified set makes an equation or inequality true.

Real World Connections

Key Words

equivalent

equation

inequality

solve an
  equation

solve an
  inequality

substitution

A restaurant offers a free dessert to all customers whose age, a, satisfies the equation $2a + 7 = 67$ or that satisfies the inequality $a + 15 \leq 21$. A family of four people dining at the restaurant have ages 35, 30, 10, and 6. How many members of that family will get a free dessert?

One way to answer that question is to use substitution and test the ages to see whether they satisfy the equation $2a + 7 = 67$ or whether they satisfy the inequality $a + 15 \leq 21$. Those steps are shown in the beginning of the *Take It Apart* section of this lesson.

Two expressions are **equivalent** if they have the same value. For example, the expressions $3(a + 2)$ and $3a + 6$ are equivalent for any value of the variable a, while the expressions $3a + 6$ and 9 are equivalent if the value of a is 1.

An **equation** is a statement that two mathematical expressions are equivalent. An **inequality** uses one of the four symbols $<$, $\leq$, $>$, or $\geq$ to describe a relationship between two expressions.

To **solve an equation** or **solve an inequality** means to find the value(s) of the variable that make the equation or inequality a true statement. For example, the value $x = 5$ is a solution to the inequality $x + 7 > 10$ because $5 + 7 > 10$ is a true statement.

The process of **substitution** means to replace a variable with a number. Examples:

Substituting 7 for x in the expression $x + 9$ results in the value $7 + 9$, or 16.

Substituting 7 for x in the equation $3x = 21$ results in the statement $3 \times 7 = 21$, which is a true statement.

Substituting 7 for x in the inequality $2x - 4 \leq 5$ results in the statement $2 \times 7 - 4 \leq 5$. That can be simplified to the inequality $10 \leq 5$, which is not a true statement.

Peoples Common Core Mathematics

Take It Apart

In the examples below, the symbol "$\stackrel{?}{=}$" is read "is [left side] equal to [right side]?" and the symbol "$\stackrel{?}{\leq}$" is read "is [left side] less than or equal to [right side]?".

Example 1: Answer the question in the Real World Connection about the ages and equation $2a + 7 = 67$.

Example 2: Answer the question in the Real World Connection about the ages and inequality $a + 15 \leq 21$.

Step 1 Write the equation: $2a + 7 = 67$

Step 2 Substitute the ages, one at a time, into the equation.

$$2(35) + 7 \stackrel{?}{=} 67$$
$$70 + 7 \stackrel{?}{=} 67 \quad \text{No}$$
$$2(30) + 7 \stackrel{?}{=} 67$$
$$60 + 7 \stackrel{?}{=} 67 \quad \text{Yes}$$
$$2(10) + 7 \stackrel{?}{=} 67$$
$$20 + 7 \stackrel{?}{=} 67 \quad \text{No}$$
$$2(6) + 7 \stackrel{?}{=} 67$$
$$12 + 7 \stackrel{?}{=} 67 \quad \text{No}$$

The value $x = 30$ satisfies the equation, so the person whose age is 30 will get a free dessert.

Step 1 Write the inequality: $a + 15 \leq 21$

Step 2 Substitute the ages, one at a time, into the inequality.

$$(35) + 15 \stackrel{?}{\leq} 21$$
$$50 \stackrel{?}{\leq} 21 \quad \text{No}$$
$$(30) + 15 \stackrel{?}{\leq} 21$$
$$45 \stackrel{?}{\leq} 21 \quad \text{No}$$
$$(10) + 15 \stackrel{?}{\leq} 21$$
$$25 \stackrel{?}{\leq} 21 \quad \text{No}$$
$$(6) + 15 \stackrel{?}{\leq} 21$$
$$21 \stackrel{?}{\leq} 21 \quad \text{Yes}$$

The value $x = 6$ satisfies the inequality, so the person whose age is 6 will get a free dessert.

Use the methods shown above to answer these questions.

1. Find the value(s) from the set {5, 7, 9, 11, 13} that satisfy the equation $4x + 3x = 77$.

   _____

2. Find the value(s) from the set {5, 7, 9, 11, 13} that satisfy the inequality $4x - 1 \leq 35$.

   _____

3. Explain how to check whether one or more values solve an equation or an inequality.

   _____

   _____

   _____

Put It Together

Use what you now know about solutions to equations and inequalities to solve these problems.

1. Which of the value(s) in the set {4, 5, 6, 7, 8} are solution(s) of the inequality $3x - 4 > 11$?

   _____

2. The equation $5x - 3 = 37$ represents the situation that you can make 37 pizzas with x pounds of flour. Which of the numbers in the set {6, 7, 8, 9} is a solution to that equation?

   _____

Answer the questions. Share your ideas with a classmate.

3. What is the least number in the set {4, 5, 6, 7, 8} that satisfies $6x - 7 > 23$? _____

4. For each equation or inequality, show the step of substituting the value of the variable. Then explain why, or why not, the value is a solution.

   a. $2x + 10 = 24$; $x = 3$

   _____

   b. $2x + 4 = 24$; $x = 10$

   _____

   b. $3(x + 5) \geq 20$; $x = 3$

   _____

   c. $3(x + 5) \geq 20$; $x = 1$

   _____

5. Which number(s) in the set {5, 10, 15, 20} satisfy both $2x = 20$ and $2x + 1 = 21$? _____

6. A student substitutes $x = 4$ into the inequality $5x \geq 20$ and finds that $x = 4$ satisfies the inequality. Do all numbers greater than 4 satisfy the inequality? Do any numbers less than 4 satisfy the inequality? Explain your answer.

   _____

   _____

   _____

Make It Work

Answer the questions below.

1. Which numbers in the set {2, 3, 4, 5} are solution(s) to the inequality $16 - 3x > 5$?

   A. 2 only   **C.** 2 and 3

   B. 3 only   **D.** 3, 4, and 5

2. Which numbers in the set {2, 3, 4, 5} are solutions to either $3x + 1 = 13$ or $\frac{x+5}{2} = 4$?

   A. 4 and 5   **C.** 2 and 4

   B. 3 and 4   **D.** 2 and 3

3. Which numbers in the set {0, 2, 4, 6, 8, 10} satisfy the inequality $3x + 5 \leq 3x + 5$? Do you have to test all the numbers? Explain.

   _____

   _____

4. Consider these three statements:

   $4x \leq 36$
   $4x = 36$
   $4x \geq 36$

   Find all the numbers that satisfy all three statements. Do you have to find solutions for the three statements separately?

   _____

   _____

   _____

5. Which numbers in the set {0, 1, 2, 3, 4} satisfy the equation $3x + 5 = 3x + 6$? Do you have to check all the values?

   _____

   _____

   _____

   _____

Lesson 32 Using Variables to Write Expressions to Solve Problems

6.EE.6 Use variables to represent numbers and write expressions when solving a real-world or mathematical problem; understand that a variable can represent an unknown number, or, depending on the purpose at hand, any number in a specified set.

Real World Connections

Key Words

verbal model

algebraic expression

Mia explained to her group in class that many times variables can be used to represent numbers in real-world situations. She demonstrated this by using the variable b to represent the final balance of a checking account. The account originally has a balance of $40. The monthly activity in the account includes three deposits of $28, $57, and $112, and one withdrawal of $37. Find the final balance at the end of the month. You can use an algebraic expression to determine the final balance in the account.

In a real-world or mathematical problem where you are trying to determine a missing amount, you can write a **verbal model** by describing the situation using only the most important words in the problem.

You should define a variable by assigning one to any unknown value in the problem. For example, if the total cost is unknown, let c represent the cost in the algebraic expression.

Once the variable has been assigned, write an **algebraic expression** that represents the situation. Use the order of operations to simplify the expression to answer the question.

The verbal model that represents the situation could be stated "the final balance is equal to the original balance plus the deposits and minus the withdrawals."

The algebraic expression $b = 40 + 28 + 57 + 112 - 37$ represents the final balance in the account. It can be simplified by following the order of operations. You can add and subtract from left to right.

$$b = 40 + 28 + 57 + 112 - 37 = 200$$

Mia said that the final balance is $200.

 ## Take It Apart

The middle school yearbook committee is charged $15 per yearbook and $19.95 for shipping per order. Write a formula that will represent the amount of money the committee will pay for any order. Determine the amount of money the committee will have to pay for an order of 25, 40, and 100 yearbooks.

Step 1 Write a verbal model that represents the situation.
Total cost is $15 times the number of yearbooks, plus $19.95 for shipping.

Step 2 Define variables to represent unknown quantities.
Let c represent total cost, and n represent the number of yearbooks purchased.

Step 3 Write a formula to represent the situation.
Total cost is $15 times the number of yearbooks, plus $19.95 for shipping.

$$c = 15 \times n + 19.95$$

Step 4 Substitute 25, 40, and 100, to find the total cost.

For 25 yearbooks	For 40 yearbooks	For 100 yearbooks
$c = 15(25) + 19.95$	$c = 15(40) + 19.95$	$c = 15(100) + 19.95$
$c = 375 + 19.95$	$c = 600 + 19.95$	$c = 1,500 + 19.95$
$c = 394.95$	$c = 619.95$	$c = 1,519.95$

The middle school yearbook committee will be charged $394.95 for 25 yearbooks, $619.95 for 40 yearbooks, and $1,519.95 for 100 yearbooks.

Answer each question.

1. A motorboat can travel 30 miles per hour in still water. The river has an unknown current flowing in the opposite direction as the boat. What is an expression that represents the speed of the boat with the current? Using distance = rate × time ($d = rt$), write an expression that represents the distance the boat travels after 3 hours. Show your work.

_____

2. A square has four sides with equal lengths. Write an expression that represents the perimeter of the square. Use the expression to find the perimeter of a square with a 5 inch side. Show your work.

_____

3. Write an expression to represent the mean of four different numbers w, x, y, and z. Explain your answer.

_____

_____

Put It Together

Answer the following questions.

1. Write an algebraic expression to represent the area of a rectangle if the length of one side is 3 and the other is *w*.

_____

2. Write an expression to represent twelve added to another number.

_____

3. Write an expression to find the total cost of 4 dozen eggs if each dozen costs *d* dollars.

_____

4. Greta wants to find the average of her last four bowling scores. What expression would you use to find the average if her scores were *n*, *n* + 4, *n* – 5, and *n* + 1? What was her average? Simplify your answer.

_____

5. If Manuel can buy *x* issues of a magazine for $75, what expression would he use to find the cost per issue?

_____

Answer the questions. Share your ideas with a classmate.

6. Why are algebraic expressions useful when solving a specific problem?

_____

_____

_____

7. There are often multiple ways to write algebraic expressions. Give an example of an expression that can be written two different ways.

_____

_____

Make It Work

Answer the questions below.

1. Mandy collects $10 from everyone who is going on the field trip. Which of the following expressions can represent this situation?

   A. $\frac{10}{x}$

   B. $10 - x$

   C. $10 + x$

   D. $10x$

2. Which expression would you use for finding the total cost of a car that sells for $6,799 with a down payment of d dollars?

   A. $6,799 + d$

   B. $6,799 - d$

   C. $6,799(d)$

   D. $\frac{6,799}{d}$

3. Write an expression for finding the perimeter of an equilateral triangle (3 sides of equal length).

   _____

4. Freddie rides his moped every Sunday afternoon. Write an expression to find how fast he rides if he can ride a certain distance in 2 hours using distance = rate × time.

   _____

   _____

5. Every year Michael's school has a jog-a-thon to raise money for the athletic program. For every lap that each student runs, $0.50 is raised. Write an expression you would use in order to find the total amount of money raised this year. Last year there were 40 more students than this year. Write an expression to represent the money raised last year.

   _____

   _____

6.EE.7   Solve real-world and mathematical problems by writing and solving equations of the form
$x + p = q$ and $px = q$ for cases in which p, q, and x are all nonnegative rational numbers.

Real World Connections

Key Words

isolate the
    variable

Additive
    Property of
    Equality

Multiplicative
    Property
    of Equality

Emma told the class that the sum of her age and her twin sister's age is 26. She explained that their ages can be found using an algebraic expression.

Since the sisters are twins, they are the same age. Their ages can, therefore, be represented by the same variable. Let a represent their ages. Set up an equation and solve to find their ages.

To solve an equation, you must follow the rules of algebra to **isolate the variable**. A variable is isolated when it is alone on one side of the equation with a coefficient of 1. You can use the Additive or Multiplicative Properties of Equality to solve equations.

The **Additive Property of Equality** allows you to keep the equation balanced by adding the same number to each side of the equation. If $a = b$, then $a + c = b + c$. You can solve an equation by adding the opposite of the number being added to the variable to both sides of the equation. For example, the opposite of 4 is -4. So,

$$x + 4 = 10$$
$$x + 4 - 4 = 10 - 4$$
$$x = 6$$

The **Multiplicative Property of Equality** allows you to keep the equation balanced by multiplying the same number to each side of the equation. If $a = b$, then $ac = bc$. You can solve an equation by multiplying the opposite of the number being multiplied by the variable on both sides of the equation. For example, the opposite of multiplying by 4 is to multiply by $\frac{1}{4}$. So,

$$4x = 12$$
$$\frac{1}{4} \cdot 4x = 12 \cdot \frac{1}{4}$$
$$x = 3$$

$a + a = 26$ Let a represent each girl's age.

$\qquad 2a = 26$ Add like terms.

$\qquad \frac{1}{2} \cdot 2a = 26 \cdot \frac{1}{2}$ Use the Multiplication Property of Equality
$\qquad\qquad\qquad\qquad$ to isolate the variable.

$\qquad a = 13$ Simplify.

Emma and her sister are each 13 years old.

Take It Apart

Jerome has a patio that currently extends 75 feet from the back of his home. This summer he plans to add to the patio so that it extends 110 feet from his home. Write an equation that represents the expansion. Solve the equation to find the length of the expansion.

Step 1 Write a verbal model that represents the situation.

The original length of the patio <u>plus</u> the expansion <u>is equal to</u> 110 feet.

Step 2 Define variables to represent unknown quantities.

Let n represent the number of feet Jerome expanded the patio.

Step 3 Write an equation to represent the expansion.

The original length of the patio <u>plus</u> the expansion <u>is equal to</u> 110 feet.
    75   + n =   110

Step 4 Use the Additive Property of Equality to solve the equation.

$$75 + n = 110$$
$$75 + n - 75 = 110 - 75$$
$$n = 35 \text{ ft}$$

Jerome is going to expand the patio 35 more feet from his home.

Answer each question.

1. A pair of jeans cost $29.96 after $1.96 tax is added to the original price. Write an equation you can use to find the original price of the jeans. Solve the equation. Show your work.

_____

_____

2. Randy can wash 2.5 more cars per hour than Johnny. Write an equation to represent the relationship between the number of cars that Randy and Johnny can wash if Randy washes 8 cars per hour. Find the number of cars Johnny can wash in an hour. Show your work.

_____

_____

3. Three-fourths a number is 45. Write an equation that represents the situation. Find the number. Show your work.

_____

Put It Together

Write an equation to find the number and solve.

1. One half of a number is 23.

_____

2. A number added to 12 is the same as 63.

_____

3. The sum of a number and 10 is 74.

_____

4. Jerrod made $3,000 less than he did last year. If he made $23,875 this year, write an equation to find what he made last year and solve.

_____

_____

5. In a school fundraiser selling candy bars, Francene sold three times as many as Gregory. If Francene sold 93 candy bars, write an equation and solve to find the number of candy bars Gregory sold.

_____

_____

Answer the question. Share your ideas with a classmate.

6. Whenever you write an equation from a word problem, what are some key words used that will help you build your equation properly?

_____

_____

Make It Work

Answer the questions below.

1. Yen puts $30 worth of gas in his truck. The price per gallon was $2.50. Which equation can be solved to find the number of gallons Yen purchased?

   A. $30g = 2.5$

   B. $\frac{30}{g} = 2.5$

   C. $30 = 2.5 + g$

   D. $30 + g = 2.5$

2. Drake buys $14 more in groceries this week than he did last week. If he spent $76 this week, choose the equation that will determine the amount he spent last week.

   A. $x + 14 = 76$

   B. $14x = 76$

   C. $76 + x = 14$

   D. $\frac{x}{76} = 14$

3. Write an equation for the following sentence and solve. Four times a number divided by three is the same as eight.

   _____

   _____

4. Jay spent ten more than three times the number of hours on his science fair project than Jesse. If Jay spent 43 hours on his project, write an equation that shows how many hours Jesse spent on his project. Solve the equation.

   _____

   _____

5. Hank and Emily work in an office building mailroom where they stuff and send envelopes. Hank can stuff 13 less than two times the amount of envelopes than Emily can stuff in a day. If Hank can stuff 225 envelopes in a day how many can Emily stuff? Write and solve an equation. If another worker Sanjay can stuff the average (mean) of Emily's and Hank's rates, how many can he stuff? Show an equation to prove your answer.

   _____

   _____

   _____

Lesson 34 Writing Inequalities to Solve Problems

6.EE.8 Write an inequality of the form $x > c$ or $x < c$ to represent a constraint or condition in a real-world or mathematical problem. Recognize that inequalities of the form $x > c$ or $x < c$ have infinitely many solutions; represent solutions of such inequalities on number line diagrams.

Real World Connections

Key Word

inequality

Mr. Meyers wanted to demonstrate the number of solutions an inequality has. To do this he discusses the age in which someone in their state must be to get their driver's license. A person must be at least 16 years old to get their license.

To help the students understand, Mr. Meyers asks a series of questions.

If you let *a* represent the age of the person, does the number sentence $a = 16$ represent the age of someone who can get their license? Why or why not? No, because people who are older than 16 can also get their license.
What type of number sentence will accurately represent the situation? an inequality
What inequality represents the situation? $a \geq 16$
How can you represent the solution? a number line

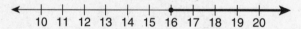

An **inequality** is a number sentence that involves $<$, $>$, $\leq$, or $\geq$. Whereas an equation (=) has one unique solution, an inequality has an infinite number of solutions. Since it is impossible to list all of the solutions of an inequality, we can use a number line to represent the solutions.

For $<$ and $>$, the solution does not include the number listed in the inequality. On the number line, these are represented by an open circle. For example,

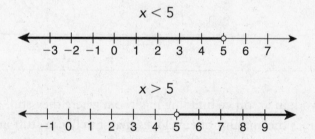

For $\leq$ and $\geq$, the solution does include the number listed in the inequality. On the number line, these are represented by a closed circle. For example,

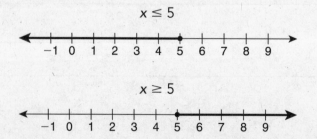

Take It Apart

Kirri has a savings account in which she wants to maintain a balance that is more than $150. Write a number sentence that represents the situation. Graph the solution.

Step 1 Define any variables. Identify key words in the problem.

Let b represent the balance of the savings account. The words "is more than" indicates that the number sentence will be an inequality with $>$.

Step 2 Write a number sentence that represents the situation.
$b > 150$

Step 3 Use a number line to graph the solution.

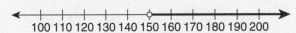

If necessary, solve the inequality showing your work. Graph the solution.

1. $n \leq -3$

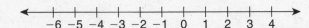

2. $x + 1 \geq 4$

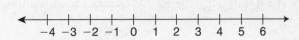

Answer each question.

1. The amusement park ride has a sign that says all riders must be a minimum of 48 inches tall. Write a number sentence to represent this situation. Graph the solution.

_____

43 44 45 46 47 48 49 50 51 52 53

2. The sign on the road indicates the speed limit is 55 miles per hour. Write a number sentence to represent this situation. Graph the solution.

_____

50 51 52 53 54 55 56 57 58 59 60

3. The menu says that children under the age of 5 eat free. Write a number sentence to represent this situation. Graph the solution.

_____

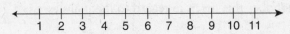

1 2 3 4 5 6 7 8 9 10 11

Put It Together

If necessary, solve the inequality showing your work. Graph the solution.

1. $y < -5$

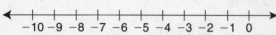

2. $a + 3 \geq 7$?

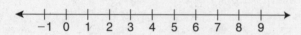

3. $3f > 12$

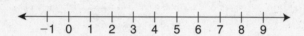

Answer the following questions.

4. Greg wants to start a glee club at his school. He wants to limit the club to students older than 12. Write a number sentence to represent the situation. Graph the solution.

_____

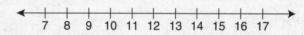

5. In a golf tournament, Rudolph shot a -7 for the tournament. He tied for first place and everyone else scored below the top two players. Write a number sentence to represent the rest of the players scores compared to Rudolph's. Graph the solution. (Note: Golf is scored by the lowest score as the best. So, no one scored less than -7.)

_____

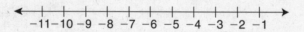

Answer the question and discuss with your classmates.

6. When looking at the graph of an inequality, how far does the number line go either way? What does this mean in regard to inequalities?

_____

_____

Make It Work

Answer the questions below.

1. The qualifying time to make it to the championship 10k race is 40 minutes. Which number sentence represents the qualifying times to make it to the championship race?

   A. $q < 40$

   B. $q > 40$

   C. $q \leq 40$

   D. $q \geq 40$

2. In the town of Destown you must be older than 18 to drive after midnight. Which number sentence represents those who can drive after midnight in the town of Destown?

   A. $a < 18$

   B. $a > 18$

   C. $a \leq 18$

   D. $a \geq 18$

3. A local rotary club only allows members that are 65 and older. Write a number sentence for the members allowed in the club. Graph the solution.

   _____

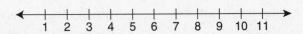

4. In order to finish her math test on time, Cheri needs to spend less than 3 minutes on each question. Write a number sentence for the time she must spend on each test question. Graph the solution.

   _____

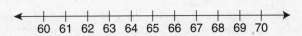

5. Kevin's Bakery has a large order for donuts before noon. He has 75 already made and he realizes that he must make more than 50 an hour to complete the order. Write a number sentence for the amount of donuts per hour he must make to complete the order. If Kevin has only three hours left, what is the minimum number of donuts he must make? Explain your reasoning.

   _____

   _____

   _____

   _____

   _____

Lesson 35 Analyzing Relationships Between Variables

6.EE.9 Use variables to represent two quantities in a real-world problem that change in relationship to one another; write an equation to express one quantity, thought of as the dependent variable, in terms of the other quantity, thought of as the independent variable. Analyze the relationship between the dependent and independent variables using graphs and tables, and relate these to the equation. *For example, in a problem involving motion at constant speed, list and graph ordered pairs of distances and times, and write the equation* $d = 65t$ *to represent the relationship between distance and time.*

Real World Connections

Toolbox

straight edge

Key Words

independent
    variable
dependent
    variable
function rule

Jennifer is raising money for the 7ᵗʰ grade class trip to Washington DC. She is participating in a swim-a-thon in which she will get paid for each lap she swims. Mrs. Jenkins has agreed to give her $2 per lap. The number of laps Jennifer swims and the money Mrs. Jenkins pays can be represented by two variables.

The variables can be defined as the dependent variable and the independent variable. The **independent variable**, or input value, is usually represented by x. The **dependent variable**, or output value, is usually represented by y. The value of the dependent variable depends on the value of the independent variable.

For example, the amount of money Mrs. Jenkins must pay depends on the number of laps Jennifer swims. Therefore, the number of laps is represented by the independent variable, x, and the amount paid by the dependent variable, y.

The relationship between the variables can be represented by an equation, or **function rule**.

Since Mrs. Jenkins will pay $2 per lap, the equation $y = 2x$ shows the relationship, where x is the number of laps and y is the amount paid.

The function rule can be used to generate several ordered pairs in a table. Begin by selecting reasonable values for the independent variable.

x (laps)	Function Rule $y = 2x$	y ($)
5	$y = 2(5)$	10
10	$y = 2(10)$	20
15	$y = 2(15)$	30

The relationship can also be represented on a graph. The ordered pairs shown in the table can be graphed onto a coordinate plane. Use a straight edge to draw the line through the points.

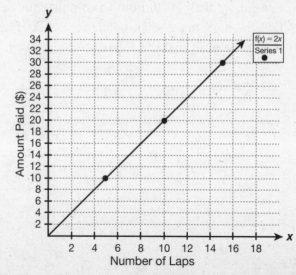

Copying is illegal.   Peoples Common Core Mathematics

Take It Apart

As a plumbing apprentice, Joe earns $16 per hour. Use variables to represent the relationship between his pay and the time he works in an equation, a table, and a graph.

Step 1 Define the independent and dependent variables.

The independent variable is the number of hours Joe works. The dependent variable is the amount of money he earns because it depends on the number of hours he works. Let x represent the number of hours worked and y the amount of money earned.

Step 2 Write an equation that represents the relationship.

Since you multiply the number of hours worked by 16 to find the amount paid, the equation is $y = 16x$

Step 3 Use the equation to create a table. Select reasonable values for x to generate ordered pairs.

x	$y = 16x$	y
10	$y = 16(10)$	160
20	$y = 16(20)$	320
40	$y = 16(40)$	640

Step 4 Use the ordered pairs to draw a graph.

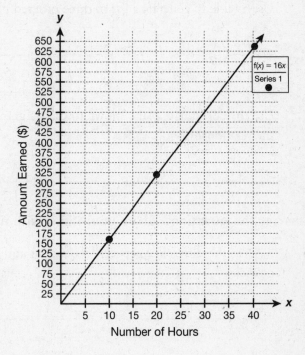

Answer each question.

1. The Iannetta's dog, Morgen, eats 1.5 cups of dog food each day. Describe the relationship between the number of days and the amount of food they need to purchase.

   a. Identify the independent and dependent variables and write a function rule that represents the relationship.

   _____

   _____

   _____

   b. Use a table to generate a list of ordered pairs.

Put It Together

Answer each question.

Jamie can crochet 3 blankets every month. Describe the relationship between the number of blankets and the time it takes her to make them.

1. Identify the dependent and independent variables.

_____

_____

2. What is the function rule that represents this relationship?

_____

3. Use a table to generate a list of three ordered pairs.

_____

_____

4. Use the coordinate plane shown to draw a graph of the relationship.

_____

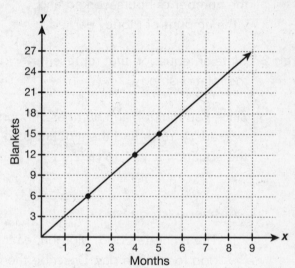

Answer the questions. Share your ideas with a classmate.

5. Discuss the difference between dependent and independent variable. Give an example of a situation of each.

_____

_____

_____

_____

6. Give an example of how you can use relationships between variables in everyday life.

_____

_____

_____

Make It Work

Answer the questions below.

1. Which of the following equations is the function rule for the ordered pairs (4, 12), (7, 21), and (11, 33)?

    A. $y = \frac{1}{3}x$

    B. $y = x + 9$

    C. $y = 3x$

    D. $y = \frac{x}{4}$

2. If the relationship between hours driven and distance traveled is $d = 45t$, which of the following ordered pairs would be graphed on the line that represents the relationship?

    A. (3, 15)

    B. (4, 60)

    C. (4, 180)

    D. (5, 9)

3. Write the function rule for the relationship shown in the graph at the right.

    _____

4. Kelli has 4 girls in her band for every boy. What are the independent and dependent variables? Explain. What is a function rule to represent the relationship?

    _____

    _____

    _____

    _____

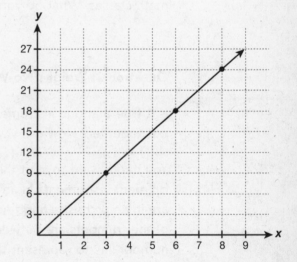

5. The Sherman Taxi Company charges $5 per mile in the city. Write a function rule to represent the relationship. Use the rule to generate three ordered pairs and graph the relationship.

    _____

    _____

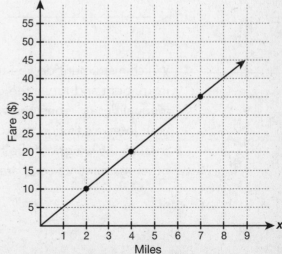

Question 1: Can You Find These Not-So-Secret Formulas?

Think about some of the formulas you have learned in your math classes. One of the most basic is the formula for the area of a rectangle, $A = l \times w$. Look through your math book, and look through textbooks for earlier grades and later grades. Can you find other formulas for area? What about formulas for volume?

Think about a way to organize, present, and explain formulas to your classmates. And don't restrict yourself to geometric formulas. Find the formula for the sum of the first n numbers: $1 + 2 + 3 + \ldots + n$. Then find the formula for the sum of the *squares* of the first n numbers, $1^2 + 2^2 + 3^3 + \ldots + n^2$. Or how about formulas for the sum of the first n triangular numbers, or for the sum of the first n pentagonal numbers? (And don't forget to explain to your classmates what "triangular numbers" and "pentagonal numbers" are as part of your presentation.)

Some people think that knowing these formulas is a formula for doing well in your math classes. What do you think?

Question 2: Weigh? No Weigh!

Is it true that one instrument in an orchestra outweighs all the other instruments put together? How can you find an answer to that question?

You might want to start this project by finding a range of weights for all the different instruments in an orchestra. For example, find out how many trumpets are in an orchestra and find a range for the weights of the trumpets. If the weights of the trumpets are between $2\frac{1}{4}$ and $3\frac{1}{4}$ pounds, you can use an interval on a number line to represent the weights of the trumpets.

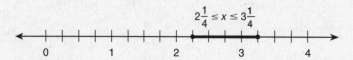

$$2\frac{1}{4} \le x \le 3\frac{1}{4}$$

Which instrument do you think is the heaviest one in an orchestra? For that instrument and for all the *other* instruments, use number line intervals and inequalities to report the weights of all the instruments. Then use the information in your intervals to find the total weight of all the other instruments, and compare that total to the weight of the heaviest instrument. How does the total weight of all the other instruments compare to the weight of the heaviest one?

Chapter 3

Question 3: Are We There Yet?

Think about planning a family car trip that will take several days or weeks. For your favorite destinations, how far is it from your home to those destinations? If you drive directly to one of the destinations, how long will the trip take? What will be your average rate of speed for the trip? If you travel on local roads, what average rates of speed will be possible? How long will the trip take for those speeds?

For the return trip home, plan a different kind of car trip. Think about how much time each day you might spend sightseeing and how many hours you would be driving. For that kind of trip, how far would you travel each day? What rates of speeds would be possible for the types of roads you would be using?

Which kind of car trip – driving directly to your destination with few stops, or sightseeing each day – do you prefer? And have a great trip!

Question 4: How Fast Is It Compared to a Car?

The next time you are in a car traveling on a highway, think about your speed. Are the dashed lane-lines going by in a blur? How fast does the car feel?

This project is about comparing other speeds to the speed of a highway-driving car. Find information about many other speeds, such as an average walking speed, or a jogging speed, or the speed of a bicyclist. How do those speeds compare to the speed of a car on a highway? How does the speed of a top marathon racer compare to a car? How about the top speed of a world-class sprinter or hurdler?

Then think about traveling faster than a car. What are the speeds for airplanes and high-speed trains? What about space shuttles?

Report your findings to your classmates. Think about how you can use charts and other displays to give a feel for the different speeds at which people travel.

6.G.1 Find the area of right triangles, other triangles, special quadrilaterals, and polygons by composing into rectangles or decomposing into triangles and other shapes; apply these techniques in the context of solving real-world and mathematical problems.

Real World Connections

Key Words

formula for
the area of
a triangle

area

formula for
the area of
a rectangle

parallelogram

triangle

base

height

formula for
the area of a
parallelogram

A new pizzeria serves "sheet pizza," which is pizza made in a rectangular pan. Two friends, sharing a pizza, order olives on one half and green peppers on the other half.

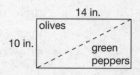

The chef decided to cut the pizza to form two right triangles. The size of the entire pizza is 10 inches by 14 inches, or 140 square inches, so the area covered by the olives is one half of 140 square inches.

In general in a right triangle, if the sides that form the right angle have lengths a and b, then this is a **formula for the area of a triangle**:

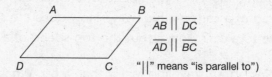

$$A = \frac{1}{2}ab$$

The **area** of a figure is the number of square units needed to cover the figure. If a rectangle has length a and width b, a **formula for the area of a rectangle** is $A = bh$.

A **parallelogram** is a figure that has two pairs of parallel sides.

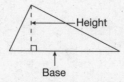

$\overline{AB} \parallel \overline{DC}$
$\overline{AD} \parallel \overline{BC}$

"$\parallel$" means "is parallel to")

A **triangle** is a figure with 3 sides. Any side can be a **base** of the triangle. The **height** for that base is the distance between the base and the opposite vertex of the triangle.

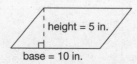

This parallelogram has a base of 10 inches and a height of 5 inches.

A **formula for the area of a parallelogram** is $A = bh$, so the area of this parallelogram is (10 inches) • (5 inches) or 50 square inches.

Take It Apart

Follow these steps to find a formula for the area of a triangle.

This right triangle has base *b* and height *h*.

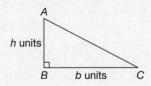

Step 1   Draw two more sides to form a rectangle.

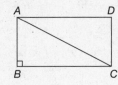

Step 2   Recall a formula for the area of the rectangle: $A = bh$.

Step 3   The triangle is exactly one-half of the rectangle, so a formula for the area of the right triangle is $A = \frac{1}{2}bh$.

This triangle has base *b* and height *h*.

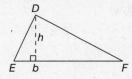

Step 1   Draw two more sides to form a parallelogram.

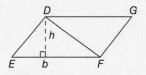

Step 2   Recall the formula for the area of a parallelogram: $A = bh$.

Step 3   The triangle is exactly one-half of the parallelogram, so a formula for the area of the triangle is $A = \frac{1}{2}bh$.

Find an expression for the area of each triangle.

1.

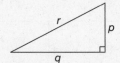

_____

2.

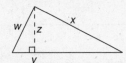

_____

3.

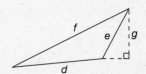

_____

4.   Refer to the *sheet pizza* at the beginning of this lesson. If the rectangular pizza is 12 inches by 18 inches, what is the area of the piece covered with green peppers?

_____

Put It Together

Find the area of each triangle.

1.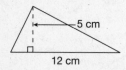

_____

2.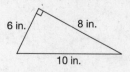

_____

3.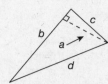

_____

4. a right triangle with sides 10, 24, and 26

_____

5.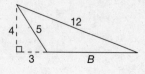

_____

6.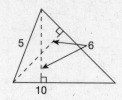

_____

Answer the questions. Share your ideas with a classmate.

7. Using a centimeter ruler, find the lengths for a base and height for this triangle. Then use the formula for the area of a triangle to find its area.

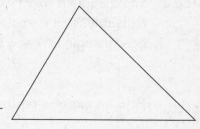

_____

_____

_____

8. On a separate sheet of graph paper, show points at A(5, 11), B(9, 3), and C(12, 11). Then explain how you can find the area of triangle ABC.

_____

_____

_____

_____

Make It Work

Answer the questions below.

1. What is the area of this triangle?

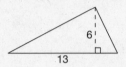

6

13

A. 19 square units   **B.** 19 $\frac{1}{2}$ square units

C. 39 square units   **D.** 78 square units

2. A garden has the shape of a right triangle. The sides of the triangle are 43 feet, 34 feet, and 26 feet. What is the area of the garden?

A. 884 square feet   **B.** 731 square feet

C. 442 square feet   **D.** 103 square feet

3. Figure *ABCD* shows a rectangle and a right triangle. Describe how the rectangle and the triangle are the same. Then tell how the area of the triangle compares to the area of the rectangle.

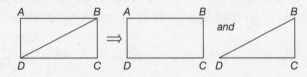

and

_____

_____

4. Use a ruler to measure the base and height of each triangle. Then find the area of each triangle.

Triangle I   Triangle II
base _____   base _____
height _____   height _____
area _____   area _____

Triangle I   Triangle II

5. A student said that if any two triangles have the same base and the same height, (such as the two triangles in question 4), then the two triangles must have the same area. Do you agree? Explain your answer.

_____

_____

_____

Lesson 37 Finding the Area of Polygons

6.G.1 Find the area of right triangles, other triangles, special quadrilaterals, and polygons by composing into rectangles or decomposing into triangles and other shapes; apply these techniques in the context of solving real-world and mathematical problems

Real World Connections

Park workers need new grass seed for the field in the park shown below. They want to purchase 1 ounce of seed for each square foot of the field.

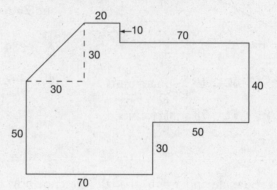

They plan to divide the field into rectangles and triangles to find the area of the field. Then they will know how much grass seed they will need.

The formula for the area of a rectangle is $A = bh$.

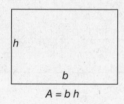

$A = b\,h$

The formula for the area of a triangle is $A = \frac{1}{2}bh$.

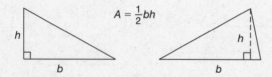

A **polygon** is a shape whose sides are straight lines. Examples of polygons are triangles, rectangles, and figures such as the field shown on this page.

   Peoples Common Core Mathematics

Take It Apart

Follow these steps to divide the field into rectangles and triangles. What is the area of the field?

Step 1 Draw 3 vertical segments and 1 horizontal segment.

Step 2 Look at the results: the figure has been divided into four rectangles and one triangle.

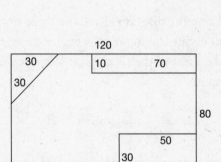

Step 3 Find the total of the areas:

$(30 \times 50) + (20 \times 80) + (70 \times 20)$
$+ (50 \times 40) + \frac{1}{2}(30 \times 30)$
$= 1,500 + 1,600 + 1,400 + 2,000 + 450$
$= 6,950$ square feet

Another way to find the area is to draw a rectangle around the original figure, then subtract the "extra" areas.

Step 1 Find the areas of the "extra" triangle and rectangles:

$\frac{1}{2}(30 \times 30) + (70 \times 10) + (30 \times 50)$
$= 450 + 700 + 1,500 = 2,650$

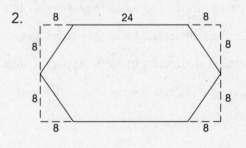

Step 2 Subtract the "extra" areas from the area of the large rectangle:

$120 \times 80 - 2,650 = 9,600 - 2,650 = 6,950.$

Use one of the strategies above to find the area of each polygon.

1.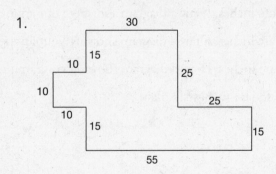

2.

_____   _____

Put It Together

Use the diagram at the right
for questions 1–3.

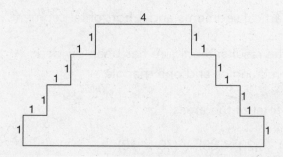

1. Copy the diagram. Then use three horizontal lines to divide the figure into four rectangles. What are the areas of the rectangles? What is the area of the figure?

_____

_____

2. Make another copy of the diagram. Then use six vertical lines to divide the figure into rectangles. What are the areas of the rectangles? What is the area of the figure?

_____

_____

3. Make another copy of the diagram and cut it out. Then cut the figure in half along a vertical line. Arrange the two parts so they form a rectangle. (Hint: You have to flip over one of the halves.) What are the dimensions of the rectangle? What is the area of the original figure?

_____

Answer the questions. Share your ideas with a classmate.

4. Carefully draw a 5-inch by 6-inch rectangle and a 4-inch by 2-inch rectangle. Then cut out the two rectangles.

   a. Arrange the rectangles so they cover an area of 38 square inches. Draw a diagram showing your arrangement.

   b. Arrange the rectangles so they cover an area of 36 square inches. Draw a diagram showing your arrangement.

   c. Arrange the rectangles so they cover an area of 30 square inches. Draw a diagram showing your arrangement.

   d. Can you arrange the two rectangles so they cover 28 square inches? Explain.

_____

_____

Make It Work

Answer the questions below.

1. What is the shaded area?

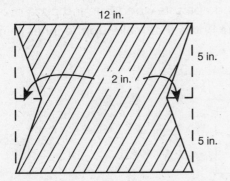

A. 60 square inches   **B.** 100 square inches

C. 120 square inches   **D.** 140 square inches

2. What is the shaded area?

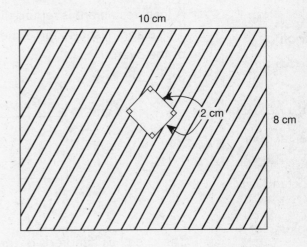

A. 76 square cm   **B.** 78 square cm

C. 80 square cm   **D.** 84 square cm

3. Describe two ways to find the area of this figure. What is the area of the figure?

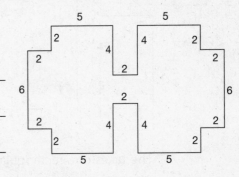

_____

_____

_____

_____

_____

4. Think about dividing a large figure into parts. How are the parts related to each other? How are the parts related to the original figure? Present your answers as a general property for area.

_____

_____

_____

_____

Lesson (38) Finding the Volume of Rectangular Prisms

6.G.2 Find the volume of a right rectangular prism with fractional edge lengths by packing it with unit cubes of the appropriate unit fraction edge lengths, and show that the volume is the same as would be found by multiplying the edge lengths of the prism. Apply the formulas $V = lwh$ and $V = bh$ to find volumes of right rectangular prisms with fractional edge lengths in the context of solving real-world and mathematical problems.

Real World Connections

A local restaurant is remodeling and taking apart its wood-burning pizza oven. This diagram shows the dimensions of the bricks that make up the inner lining of the oven.

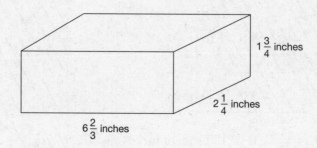

$1\frac{3}{4}$ inches

$2\frac{1}{4}$ inches

$6\frac{2}{3}$ inches

The oven has hundreds of these bricks, and the restaurant owners need to identify enough space to store the bricks until they can rebuild their oven.

A **rectangular prism** or a **rectangular solid** is a solid figure in which all six faces are rectangles; it looks like a box.

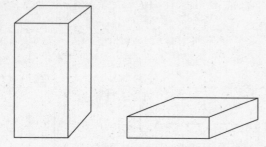

The faces of a rectangular prism are rectangles. In any rectangular prism, opposite faces are parallel and have the same size and shape. At each corner or vertex of a rectangular prism, three faces meet and each one is perpendicular to the other two.

The **volume of a rectangular prism** is the amount of space that the prism takes up. Here are two formulas for the volume of a rectangular prism.

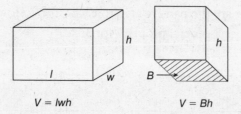

$V = lwh$ $V = Bh$

The formula on the left uses the three dimensions of a rectangular prism, its **length**, **width**, and **height**. The formula on the right uses the **base**, which is the product of two of the dimensions, and the height.

Toolbox

calculator

Key Words

rectangular prism

rectangular solid

volume of a rectangular prism

length

width

height

base

Take It Apart

The measurement for the length, width, and height of this rectangular prism are mixed numbers. Here are three methods to find the volume of the prism.

Method 1: Use a calculator that works with fractions.

Step 1 Use the formula $V = lwh$, and enter $5\frac{3}{4} \times 3\frac{1}{3} \times 7\frac{1}{2}$.

Step 2 Record the result: $143\frac{3}{4}$ cubic units.

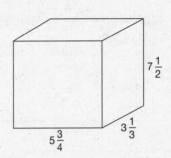

Method 2: Use mental math to convert each mixed number to a decimal.

Step 1 Mentally convert $7\frac{1}{2}$, $5\frac{3}{4}$, and $3\frac{1}{3}$ to 7.5, 5.75, and 3.333, respectively.

Step 2 Use a calculator or pencil and paper to calculate: $(7.5) \times (5.75) \times (3.333) = 143.74$.

Step 3 Record the result: 143.74 cubic units.

Method 3: Use the parenthesis keys on your calculator to convert each mixed number to a decimal.

Step 1 Keyboard the key sequence $(7 + 1 \div 2) \times (5 + 3 \div 4) \times (3 + 1 \div 3) =$

Step 2 The display should show 143.75.

Step 3 Record the result: 143.75 cubic units.

Use one of the methods shown above to find each volume.

1.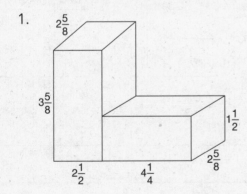

2. The restaurant owners tied the bricks in packages of 4.

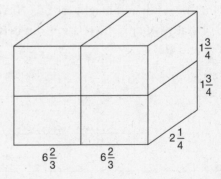

Find the volume of each package of 4 bricks.

Put It Together

Use what you know about rectangular prisms to find the following volumes.

1. A rectangular prism is $13\frac{7}{8}$ inches long, $5\frac{3}{4}$ inches wide, and $4\frac{3}{8}$ inches tall. What is the volume of the prism?

_____

_____

2. Find the volume of this rectangular prism.

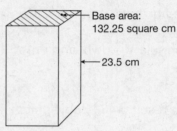

Base area: 132.25 square cm

23.5 cm

3. What is the volume of the rectangular prism shown at the right? Use the formula $V = Bh$ and use the shaded face as the base. Show your work.

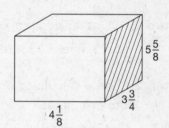

$5\frac{5}{8}$

$3\frac{3}{4}$

$4\frac{1}{8}$

_____

_____

Answer the question. Share your ideas with a classmate.

4. Box A has dimensions l, w, and h. Box B has dimensions $2l$, $2w$, and $2h$. Assign values for l, w, and h for Box A. What is the volume of Box A for your values? Using your values for Box A, tell the length, width, and height for Box B. What is the volume of Box B? Finally, what is the relationship between the volumes of boxes A and B?

A

l

h

w

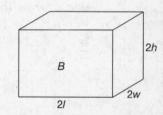

B

$2h$

$2l$

$2w$

_____

_____

_____

Make It Work

Answer the questions below.

1. Which expression does not represent the volume of this rectangular prism?

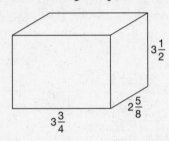

$3\frac{1}{2}$

$2\frac{5}{8}$

$3\frac{3}{4}$

A. $9\frac{3}{16} \times 3\frac{3}{4}$ **B.** $9\frac{7}{8} \times 2\frac{5}{8}$

C. $9\frac{27}{32} \times 3\frac{1}{2}$ **D.** $13\frac{1}{8} \times 2\frac{5}{8}$

2. The volume of rectangular prism P is four times the volume of rectangular prism with dimensions $2\frac{3}{4}$, $3\frac{1}{4}$, and $3\frac{1}{2}$. Which set of dimensions can represent prism P?

   A. $2\frac{3}{4}$ by $3\frac{1}{4}$ by 7   **B.** $2\frac{3}{4}$ by $6\frac{1}{2}$ by 7

   C. $5\frac{1}{2}$ by $3\frac{1}{4}$ by $3\frac{1}{2}$ **D.** $5\frac{1}{2}$ by $6\frac{1}{2}$ by 7

3. Refer to the bricks from the Real World Connection. If 100 of the bricks are placed together on the ground so that they are all resting on the face that has dimensions $1\frac{3}{4}$ by $2\frac{1}{4}$, what area is covered by the 100 bricks? If that area represents a base for a rectangular prism that contains 1,000 bricks, what is the height of that prism?

_____

_____

4. Suppose a crate has a volume of 24 cubic feet and a trunk has a capacity of 24 cubic feet. Explain the difference between volume and capacity. Can the crate fit inside the trunk? Can the trunk fit inside the crate? Explain.

_____

_____

_____

_____

Lesson 39 Drawing Polygons in the Coordinate Plane

6.G.3 Draw polygons in the coordinate plane given coordinates for the vertices; use coordinates to find the length of a side joining points with the same first coordinate or the same second coordinate. Apply these techniques in the context of solving real-world and mathematical problems.

Real World Connections

A city is organizing a Sunday race using north-south streets and east-west streets. After imposing a grid over the city streets, the planners decided the racers would begin at *A*(0, 0), then proceed to points *B*(0, 20), *C*(40, 20), *D*(40 −10), *E*(−30, −10), *F*(−30, 0), and end back at *A*(0, 0).

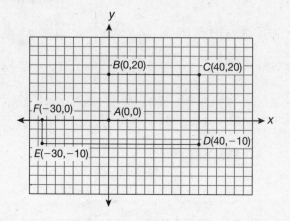

A **coordinate plane** or **coordinate grid** is a grid determined by two number lines, or **axes**, that intersect at their zero points.

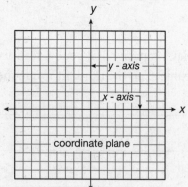

Each point in the grid is associated with an **ordered pair (x, y)**, where x represents the horizontal distance from (0, 0) and y represents the vertical distance from (0, 0).

On the **horizontal axis**, positive values represent locations to the right of zero and negative values represent locations to the left of zero. For the **vertical axis**, zero and up is positive and zero and down is negative.

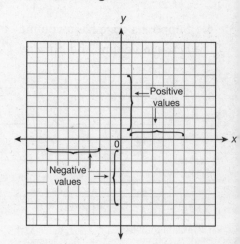

Take It Apart

The two axes for this graph indicate distances in city blocks. Here are two methods to find the distance between C(40, 20) and D(40, −10).

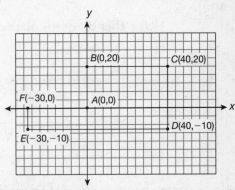

Method 1: Count blocks.

Step 1 Begin at C(40, 20). Count the number of blocks, along a vertical line, from C to the x-axis. There are 20 blocks from C to the x-axis.

Step 2 Staying on the same vertical line, count the number of blocks from the x-axis to D(40, −10). There are 10 blocks from the x-axis to D(40, −10).

Step 3 Add the two numbers: 20 + 10 = 30. The distance between C(40, 20) and D(40, −10) is 30 blocks.

Method 2: Subtract the two coordinates that are not the same.

Step 1 Identify the two coordinates that are not the same: 20 and −10.

Step 2 Set up a subtraction expression: 20 − (−10).

Step 3 Simplify the expression: 20 − (−10) = 30. Again, the distance is 30.

Use one of the methods above to find distances on this map. Each unit on the graph represents 1 meter.

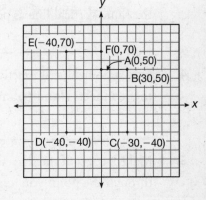

1. From E to D

   _____

2. Between D and C

   _____

3. From A to B, and then to C

   _____

4. From A to B, to C, to D, to E, to F, and then back to A

   _____

5. Using the same graph as in question 4, suppose you begin at point C and then go to points D, E, F, A, B, and end at C. What is the total distance? Do you have to do any calculations?

   _____

6. Look at Method 2. Explain what happens if you use subtraction to find the distance between D(40, −10) and C(40, 20). How can you use absolute value and subtraction to find the distance?

   _____

   _____

   _____

Put It Together

Use this diagram at the right for questions 1–5.

1. Is point *Q* closer to point *P* or to point *R*? Justify your answer.

   _____

   _____

   _____

2. Find and name the coordinates of a point that is on the same vertical line as point *R* and that is 10 units from point *R*.

   _____

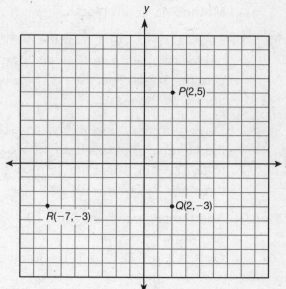

Answer the questions. Share your ideas with a classmate.

3. Find the coordinates of four points that are 12 units from point *P*. (*Hint*: Find two points that are on the same horizontal line as point *P* and find two points that are on the same vertical line as point *P*.)

   _____

4. Find a point that is exactly halfway between points *P* and *Q*. (Hint: Copy the diagram and draw the segment that connects *P* and *Q*, and find the midpoint of that segment.

   _____

5. Make a copy of the diagram showing points *P*(2, 5) and *Q*(2, −3). On your copy, show a horizontal line through the point you found in question 4.

   a. What angle is formed by segment $\overline{PQ}$ and your horizontal line?

   _____

   b. Select a point on your horizontal line, and measure the distance form your point to points *P* and *Q*. What seems to be true about the two distances?

   _____

   c. Do you get the same result as part b for every point on your horizontal line?

   _____

Make It Work

Answer the questions below.

For questions 1-2, use the diagram below.

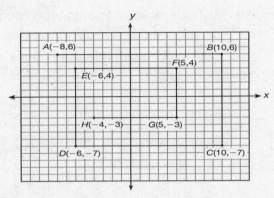

1. What is the distance between points *E* and *F*?

   A. −1 unit   **B.** 1 unit

   C. 8 units   **D.** 11 units

2. Which segment has the longest length?

   A. $\overline{AB}$ **B.** $\overline{BC}$

   C. $\overline{CD}$ **D.** $\overline{DE}$

3. Show that the perimeters of figure *PQRSTUVW* and figure *ABCD* are the same. Explain why the perimeters have to be the same. (Hint: Separate each perimeter into the lengths of the horizontal sides and the lengths of the vertical sides.

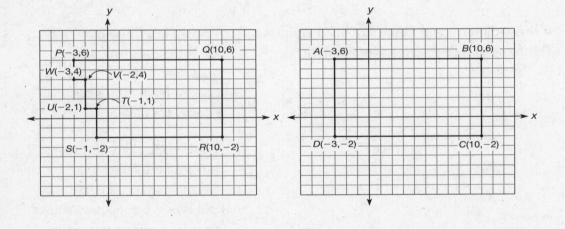

_____

_____

_____

_____

_____

_____

Lesson 40 Representing Three-Dimensional Figures Using Nets

6.G.4 Represent three-dimensional figures using nets made up of rectangles and triangles, and use the nets to find the surface area of these figures. Apply these techniques in the context of solving real-world and mathematical problems

Real World Connections

The company *Present Tents* makes camping tents, party tents, all different kinds and sizes of tents. Someone in the company's Art Department makes a drawing of the tent. Then the Production Department "opens up" the tent so they can figure out how much canvas they need and how to manufacture the tent.

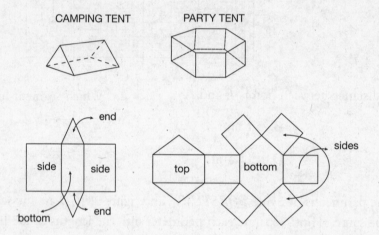

Key Words

three-dimensional figure

faces

prism

base

net

triangular prism

hexagonal prism

A **three-dimensional figure** is a solid figure. The **faces** of a three-dimensional figure may be flat or curved.

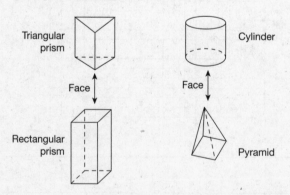

A **prism** is a three-dimensional figure that has two parallel faces. Each of those faces is called a **base**. The sides of a prism are rectangles.

A **net** is a flat drawing that shows all the faces of a three-dimensional figure. The Real World Connection shows a net for a **triangular prism** (a prism with a triangle as each base) and a **hexagonal prism** (a prism with a hexagon as each base).

 Peoples Common Core Mathematics

Take It Apart

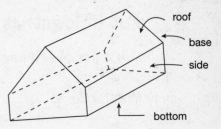

There are many different ways to draw a net for any solid figure. The test for any net is that it can be cut out and folded to form that solid figure. Every net for the solid figure above should have 7 faces, consisting of 5 rectangles and 2 pentagons.

You can follow these steps to make a net for the solid figure shown at the right. Each of the two 5-sided faces is labeled "base" because in a prism, the bases are the faces that are parallel to each other.

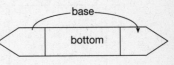

Step 1 Start with any one of the faces. It is often easiest to start with the "bottom" face. Then show how the two parallel bases can be related to the bottom face.

Step 2 The bottom is also connected to the two faces labeled "side." The two faces labeled "roof" are connected to the sides.

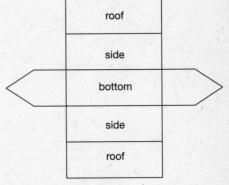

Use the method above, or your own method, to draw a net for each solid figure.

1.

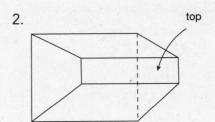

2.   top

 Put It Together

Use a pencil and paper for these questions.

1. Draw a net for this solid.

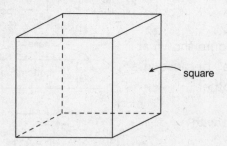

square

2. A *cube* is a prism in which all six faces are squares. Draw a net for a cube.

3. Draw a net for this prism, in which the bases are right triangles.

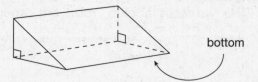

bottom

4. An *equilateral triangular* prism has bases that are equilateral triangles (three equal sides). Draw a net for an equilateral triangular prism.

 Peoples Common Core Mathematics

Make It Work

Answer the questions below.

1. Which solid figure can be made from this net?

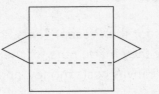

   A.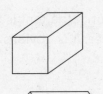

   B.

   C.

   D.

2. A net for a solid figure consists of 2 triangles and 3 rectangles. Which of the following is the best name for the solid figure?

   A. triangular net

   B. triangular prism

   C. triangular pyramid

   D. rectangular prism

3. A student begins drawing a net for a triangular prism by drawing one of the bases. What is the shape of that base? How many other faces for the net can be shown sharing an edge with that base? How many faces of the net cannot share an edge with that base?

   _____

   _____

4. This net can be folded to make an "open box," which is a box with no top face. What are all the ways to add one more square to the net so the new diagram is a net for a cube? For each of your nets, use an "X" to match the X in the given diagram and shade your "new" square.

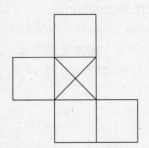

Lesson 41 — Using Nets to Find the Surface Area of Three-Dimensional Figures

6.G.4 Represent three-dimensional figures using nets made up of rectangles and triangles, and use the nets to find the surface area of these figures. Apply these techniques in the context of solving real-world and mathematical problems

Real World Connections

Key Words

prism

bases

pyramid

net

surface area

On their first day as interns for the *Present Tents* Production Department, the interns were asked why they made nets for their tents. One intern raised her hand and suggested that "canvas costs money, and the net helps you find ways to reduce waste."

Below are the company's Camping Tent and two nets for the tent. If the tent is made by cutting the net from a single rectangular sheet of canvas, it is obvious that one net can start with a smaller rectangle than the other.

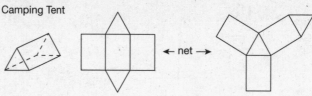

Camping Tent ← net →

A **prism** has at least two faces that are parallel. Those two faces are called the **bases** of the prism. The shape of every other face of a prism is a rectangle.

A **pyramid** is a three-dimensional figure that has one base. The rest of the faces of a pyramid are triangles that all meet at a single point. A pyramid is named by the shape of its base.

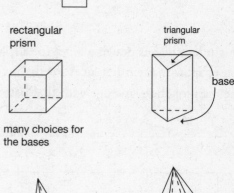

rectangular prism

triangular prism

base

many choices for the bases

square pyramid

hexagonal pyramid

A **net** is a flat drawing that shows all the faces of a three-dimensional figure. The **surface area** of a three-dimensional figure is the total area of all the faces of the figure. To find the surface area of a figure, draw a net for the figure and find the area of each part of the net. There are usually many ways to draw a net for a particular three-dimensional figure.

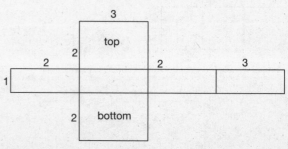

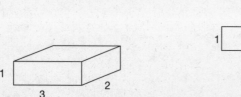

Surface Area: $2(2 \times 3) + 2(2 \times 1) + 2(3 \times 1) = 22$ units^2

Peoples Common Core Mathematics

 ## Take It Apart

This diagram shows two different nets for the Camping Tent. Each net is shown inside a large rectangle. Find the area of the net. Then find the area of the canvas that is not used for each net.

Figure 1

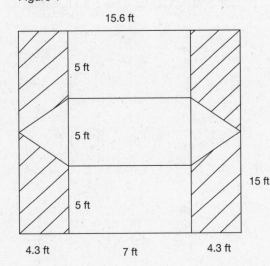

Figure 2

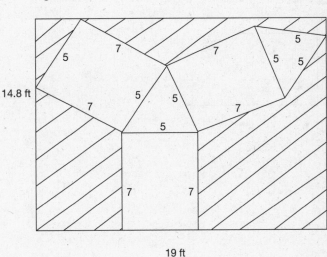

Step 1 The net is made up of three same-size rectangles and two same-size triangles. Use the formulas for the area of a rectangle and the area of a triangle to find the area of the net.

There are 3 rectangles and 2 triangles.
Area of rectangles = l x w
Area of triangles = 1/2 (b x h)

$$3 \text{ rectangles} + 2 \text{ triangles}$$
$$3(l \times w) + 2(\tfrac{1}{2} \times b \times h)$$
$$3(5 \times 7) + 2(\tfrac{1}{2} \times 5 \times 4.3)$$
$$105 + 21.5 = 126.5 \text{ square feet}$$

Step 2 Subtract the area of the net from the large rectangle.

Figure 1: (15.6 × 15) − 126.5 = 234 − 126.5 = 107.5
Figure 2: (19.6 × 14.8) − 126.5 = 290 − 126.5 = 63.5

The plan shown above on the left has much less waste.

Put It Together

Draw a net for each solid figure. Then use your net to find the surface area of the figure.

1.

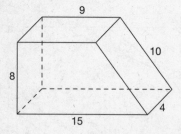

2. a cube with edges that are 3 inches long

3. Refer to the net for the Party Tent on the first page of Lesson 40. If each side of the tent is a 10-foot by 12-foot rectangle, and the area of the top (and bottom) of the tent is 260 square feet, what is the total surface area of the tent?

4. The figure shown here, made out of wood, has 5 faces. Each face is either a rectangle or a right triangle. It is going to be placed so one of the 5 faces is on the ground. Then all the faces except the one on the ground will be painted.

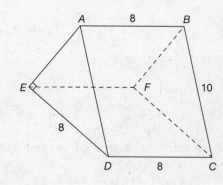

a. List the 5 faces. (For a start, the "back" of the figure as it appears above is *ABFE*.)

b. Assume that each of the 5 faces, one at a time, is on the ground. Find the area of the remaining 4 faces that would need to be painted.

Make It Work

Answer the questions below.

1. What is the area of this net?

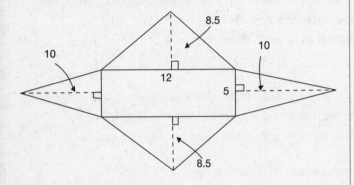

   8.5

10

   10

12

5

   8.5

  A. 85 square units   **B.** 152 square units

  C. 212 square units   **D.** 364 square units

2. Which figure has a net like the one in question 1?

  A. a rectangular prism

  B. a rectangular pyramid

  C. a square pyramid

  D. a triangular pyramid

3. The two rectangular prisms, *A* and *B*, are glued together to become prism *C*. When prisms *A* and *B* are separate, how does their total surface area compare to the surface area of prism *C*? Explain your answer. Then confirm your answer by finding the surface areas of prisms *A*, *B*, and *C*.

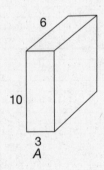

6

10

3

A

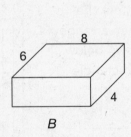

8

6

4

B

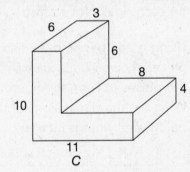

3

6

6

8

10

4

11

C

_____

_____

_____

_____

Question 1: Can you double?

You probably know many ways to find the area of a square. You can measure a side in inches or centimeters, and then calculate the area. Or you can use a grid square, of any size, and see how many of those units are needed to cover your square. Or, the easiest way: if you use your square as a unit, then the area of your square is "one square unit"!

Can you double a square? That is, draw any square. Then draw another square that has an *area* that is exactly two times the area of your original square. Explain how you can find a square whose area is exactly two times the area of a given square.

Is that too easy? Then try it with a cube! Draw a net for an open-top cube. Then draw a net for another open-top cube so the new cube has exactly two times the *capacity* or *volume* of the given cube. You can use rice or sand to see if two scoops with the first cube will exactly fill the second cube.

Question 2: Who do you believe, your eyes or your math?

What is the area of a square that is 8 inches on each side? Not so fast!

Using graph paper, draw and cut out the pieces shown in this diagram. Then arrange the pieces to form the figure shown below. What are the dimensions of the rectangle below, and what is its area?

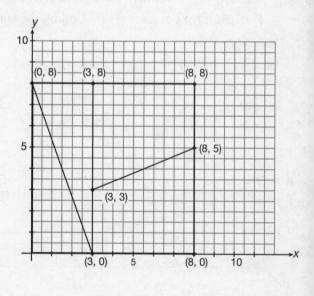

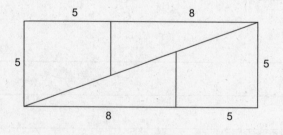

But wait! The four pieces originally have an area of 64 square units. If you make a very careful version of the 4 pieces from the coordinate grid, can you explain what's going on?

 Question 3: What does a "wall net" of your room look like?

A student used the term "wall net" to describe a diagram of her room – just the four walls, without the ceiling or the floor.

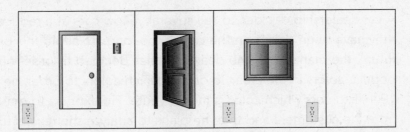

Draw a "wall net" for the walls of a room in your home or in your school. Make careful measurements and put in the doors, windows, outlets, light switches, and any other things attached to the walls. Describe how you can use your "wall net" for these questions:

○ How much wood trim would you need to cover all the edges where the walls and ceiling meet?

○ How many square feet of windows are there?

○ How can you find the area of the room's floor?

○ What is the ratio of window area to floor area?

What else can you do with your "wall net"?

 Question 4: Does "footprint" matter in grocery store packages?

A company that packages laundry detergent uses the front face of the box for advertising. Also, they want the box to have a big-enough footprint, or base, so the box is stable on the shelf.

Can you help the company? What are some different sizes for boxes that have a volume of 216 cubic inches? Make a net for your boxes, and label the *front* and *footprint* for each box.

The company knows that the cost to make each box depends on the total surface area of the box. Find the surface area for each net.

Can you recommend a particular box to the company? What area does the box have for advertising? Does the box seem stable on its base? What is the surface area of the box?

6.SP.1 Recognize a statistical question as one that anticipates variability in the data related to the question and accounts for it in the answers. *For example, "How old am I?" is not a statistical question, but "How old are the students in my school?" is a statistical question because one anticipates variability in students' ages.*

Real World Connections

Key Words

statistical
    question

surveys

data

population

sample

A car dealership decides to sell several yellow cars at a reduced price because they have been sitting on the car lot too long. To avoid this problem in the future, the manager of the dealership has decided to order only the four most popular colors in the area. To decide which colors to order, he will ask the next 100 customers which color is their favorite. He expects to get a variety of answers from the customers and then he plans to analyze the results to make his final decision.

A **statistical question** is one in which you expect the answers to vary. Statistical questions can be asked through a variety of methods, such as written questionnaires, called **surveys**, verbal polls or interviews, or even online questionnaires.

The information gathered from the answers to statistical questions is called **data** and the group from which the data was gathered is called the **population**. When you want to know information about a very large population, you can survey a smaller portion of the population, called a **sample**.

When creating a survey or poll, it is very important to word the questions so that the data gathered will be useful and can be analyzed. For example, if you would like to know the most common color car of your classmates, you might ask "What is your favorite color car?" but you would NOT ask "Do you like blue cars?"

Take It Apart

A shoe company wrote the survey at the right. They plan to give it to sixth graders each time the company designs a new shoe. Which question on the survey is not a statistical question?

Step 1 Read each question carefully and determine whether you would expect the answers to vary. In other words, would you expect every sixth grader to answer the question in exactly the same way or in different ways?

Question 1: No, the answers would most likely not vary.
Question 2: Yes, the answers would most likely vary.
Question 3: Yes, the answers would most likely vary.
Question 4: Yes, the answers would most likely vary.
Question 5: Yes, the answers would most likely vary.

> 6th Grade Shoe Survey
> 1. Do you own a pair of shoes?
> 2. How many pairs of shoes do you own?
> 3. What is your favorite color of shoe?
> 4. Do you prefer shoes, sandals, or boots?
> 5. How much are you willing to pay for a pair of shoes?

Step 2 Choose the question for which you would not expect the answers to vary. This question is not a statistical question.

"Do you own a pair of shoes?" is not a statistical question because you would expect every sixth grader to answer the same way (Yes).

A car company wrote a survey to find out what sixth graders think about different aspects of cars. Use the strategy above to determine whether each of the questions is a statistical question based on a population of sixth graders. Answer Yes or No.

1. What is your favorite color car?

   _____

2. Do you have a driver's license?

   _____

3. How much should a new car cost?

   _____

4. Which do you like best: a truck, car, or SUV?

   _____

5. How many cars do your family own?

   _____

6. In the state in which you live, how old do you have to be to get a driver's license?

   _____

Put It Together

A new employer in the area decided to consider hiring high school seniors. The company conducted a survey of all seniors at the local high schools that included each of the questions below. Use what you now know to decide whether each question is a statistical question in this situation.

1. Do you own a car?

   _____

2. Do you have a college degree?

   _____

3. How old were you when you had your first job?

   _____

4. Were you born before 1990?

   _____

5. What is your favorite hobby?

   _____

6. Do you currently have a job?

   _____

Answer each question.

7. In a survey question, explain what it means to say that you expect the answers to vary.

   _____

   _____

8. You are designing a survey for sixth graders about their study habits. Write three statistical questions that you might include on the survey.

   _____

   _____

   _____

       Peoples Common Core Mathematics

Make It Work

Answer the questions below.

1. If each of the following questions were asked to a group of second graders, which question would not be a statistical question?

   A. What time do you wake up in the morning?

   B. How tall are you?

   C. How many brothers and sisters do you have?

   D. What grade are you in?

2. For which population would the following question not be a statistical question?

   "How many days per week do you drive to work?"

   A   all the parents at a PTA meeting

   B.   Mr. Smith's first grade class

   C.   Mrs. Kadel's eleventh grade class

   D.   everyone at a movie theater

3. A company has developed a new type of pesticide that will help control algae in ponds. Before they can sell the pesticide, they must determine whether the pesticide will harm the fish in the ponds. They decide to survey pond owners about the kind of fish in the area. Write an example of a question that might be on the survey but is not a statistical question.

   _____

   _____

4. Explain why the questions on a history quiz about dates of major events would most likely not be considered statistical questions, even though some students may give different answers than others.

   _____

   _____

5. Is it possible for a particular question, such as "Do you own a pair of shoes?" to be a statistical question for one population, but not for a different population? Explain your reasoning.

   _____

   _____

   _____

Lesson 43 Describing Sets of Data

6.SP.2   Understand that a set of data collected to answer a statistical question has a distribution which can be described by its center, spread, and overall shape.

6.SP.3   Recognize that a measure of center for a numerical data set summarizes all of its values with a single number, while a measure of variation describes how its values vary with a single number.

Real World Connections

Toolbox

calculator

Key Words

distribution

central
   tendency

mean

median

mode

range

variation

skewed

News reports are full of statistics every day: batting averages, unemployment rates, rainfall amounts, movie sales, and on and on. In most cases, lots of data has been collected, analyzed, and then summarized so that it will not only make sense to the public, but also so that it will have an impact on the public.

The **distribution** of a data set is an arrangement of its values showing how often the values occurred. Distribution can be described by the center, spread, or overall shape of the data.

The center of a distribution is described using measures of **central tendency**. The **mean** is the sum of the numbers of a data set divided by the number of data items. The **median** is the middle number when the numbers are ordered from least to greatest. If there is an even number of values, the median is the mean, or average, of the two middle numbers. If there is an odd number of values, the median is the middle number in the ordered list when the numbers are sorted from lowest to highest. The **mode** is the number or numbers that occur most often.

The **range** is another measure that is often used to describe a set of data. The range is the difference between the greatest and least numbers.

Variation describes how far the data points lie away from the mean of the data. It is a measure of the data's spread. It is not a summary of the numbers, but rather a comparison between each data point and the mean of the data.

Data can have a variety of shapes. Three common shapes are shown here.

In a data set that is **skewed**, most of the data lies to one side or the other of the mean, rather than in the middle with the mean.

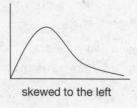

skewed to the left

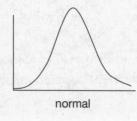

normal

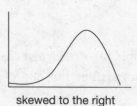

skewed to the right

178   Mathematics • Level F   Copying is illegal.   Peoples Common Core Mathematics

 ## Take It Apart

Use mean, median, and mode to describe the set of data below that represents the number of strikeouts in a single game that a new pitcher in the major leagues threw during his first eight games.

$$12, 8, 5, 9, 10, 4, 7, 9$$

Step 1 Order the data values from least to greatest.

$$4, 5, 7, 8, 9, 9, 10, 12$$

Step 2 Find the mean by adding the values and then dividing by the number of values.

$$\frac{4 + 5 + 7 + 8 + 9 + 9 + 10 + 12}{8} = \frac{64}{8} = 8$$

Step 3 Find the median by locating the number in the middle. Since there is an even number of values, find the average of the two middle numbers.

$$\frac{8 + 9}{2} = \frac{17}{2} = 8.5$$

Step 4 Find the mode by locating the number that occurs more often.

The mode is 9 since it is the only number that occurs more often.

Use the strategies above to find the mean, median, and mode of the data for each situation.

1. Daniela bowled the following scores:
   125, 140, 97, 140, 132, 128.

   _____

   _____

   _____

2. Damian scored 74, 75, 75, 80, and 76 on his five most recent math tests.

   _____

   _____

   _____

3. Prices for the main entrees at Michelle's Restaurant are: $18, $16, $25, $27, $19, $26, and $16.

   _____

   _____

   _____

4. The high temperatures for the week were:
   84, 80, 88, 90, 87, 85, 88.

   _____

   _____

   _____

Put It Together

Use what you now know about mean, median, and mode to describe the following sets of data.

1. Carla is getting ready for a recital. The numbers of hours that Carla practiced the flute each week last month were: 7, 12, 5, and 8.

_____

_____

_____

2. The rainfall per day over the past week in inches was: 2, 0, 2, 5, 0, 3, 2

_____

_____

_____

Answer each question.

3. Juanita's teacher told her parents that she was a very consistent test-taker. Her test grades for the six-week grading period were 90, 88, 93, 89, and 90. Explain why the range of the data would support the teacher's comment.

_____

_____

_____

4. The manager of a women's shoe store recorded the shoe size for the first 100 customers that came into the store. The graph at the right shows a summary of the data. Use the shape of the graph to estimate the percent of the next shoe order that should be size 8 and explain your reasoning.

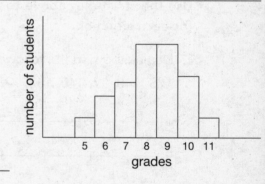

_____

_____

_____

5. Explain the difference between measures of central tendency and variation.

_____

_____

_____

Make It Work

Answer the questions below.

1. Mean, median, and mode are summary numbers that measure what aspect of a set of data?

   A. the highest value

   B. the frequency

   C. the center

   D. the number of observations

2. Which statistical measure is not a summary number, but rather a comparison between each data value and a single number?

   A. variation

   B. mean

   C. median

   D. mode

Answer each question.

3. Which statistical measure, the mean, median, mode, or range, has the greatest value for the set of data below? Support your answer using specific values. 54, 66, 56, 84, 66, and 34

   _____

   _____

4. The tenth grade statistics teacher plotted the distribution of grades on the last test. The graph is shown at the right. Describe the overall shape of the distribution and then write a sentence that summarizes the performance of the class based on the shape.

   _____

   _____

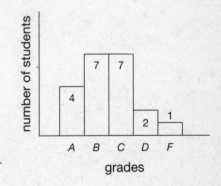

5. What letter grade represents the median of the data in problem 4? Explain your reasoning.

   _____

   _____

   _____

6.SP.4	Display numerical data in plots on a number line, including dot plots, histograms, and box plots.
6.SP.5.c	Giving quantitative measures of center (median and/or mean) and variability (interquartile range and/or mean absolute deviation), as well as describing any overall pattern and any striking deviations from the overall pattern with reference to the context in which the data were gathered.

Real World Connections

Key Words

dot plot

outlier

A shoe company polled 25 sixth-graders to determine what price they believe is appropriate for a pair of every-day tennis shoes. The students could choose any price between $15 and $50, in multiples of $5. The results of the poll are shown in the tally chart at the right. The manager of the shoe company would like to display the data in a simple, visual chart to help make pricing decisions.

Sixth Grade Poll on Pricing

Price	Students
$15	I
$20	₩
$25	₩ ₩
$30	₩ I
$35	I
$40	
$45	
$50	II

There are lots of ways to effectively display statistical data. For example, data can be displayed in dot plots, line graphs, histograms, box plots, stem-and-leaf plots, or circle graphs. To determine which type of plot is best for a set of data, several things should be considered. For example, it is important to consider the purpose of the display, how much data there is to be displayed, and the nature of the data being investigated.

A **dot plot** is a type of chart that uses a number line and groups of dots to represent data points. It is one of the simplest statistical plots and is suitable only for small-to-medium size data sets. Here is an example of a dot plot.

First Twenty Customers of the Day

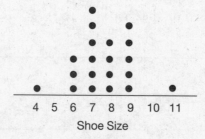

Shoe Size

A dot plot is easy to read visually and is especially useful for identifying clusters of data, gaps in the data, and outliers. An **outlier** is a data point that is markedly lesser or more than the other data points. In the dot plot above, you can see a cluster above sizes 6, 7, 8, and 9 and two outliers at sizes 4 and 11. Information like this would be important for a store manager when deciding what size shoes to order for the store.

Take It Apart

To display the results of the shoe company's poll in a dot plot, follow some simple steps.

Step 1 Set up the graph.

Choose an appropriate title.
Label the number line based on the data,
in this case the shoe prices. Do not skip values.
It is important to be able to see clusters and gaps.

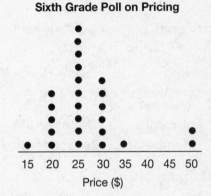

Sixth Grade Poll on Pricing

Step 2 Count the number of marks for each price
in the tally chart. Place the same number
of dots above the price on the number line.

Step 3 Identify any clusters and/or outliers. Draw conclusions
from this information.

There is a cluster around the prices $20, $25, and $30. This might be a good price range
for different styles of shoes. There are two outliers at $50. This might indicate that some
students would pay more, perhaps if there were something special about the shoes.

Use the strategy above to display the set of data in a dot plot. Then answer the question.

1. A math teacher polled her students to see how many questions they would prefer
   to see on a math test. She reminded them that the more questions there are, the less
   each one counts. The results are shown in the tally chart.

Questions	Students
5	I
10	IIII
15	I
20	IJH IJH
25	IJH III
30	I

2. Based on the display, if the teacher wants to please as many students as possible,
   how many questions should she put on her next two tests? Explain your reasoning.

_____

_____

_____

Lesson 44 Displaying Data in Number Lines and Dot Plots

Put It Together

Use what you now know about dot plots to display the set of data below in a simple visual plot.

1. A water park is trying to decide how many seats to put in its new raft. The raft will be used in a ride intended for the whole family. The manager of the water park polls the first 35 families to enter the park regardless of how many people are in their family. The results are shown in the tally chart. Display the data in a dot plot.

Number of Family Members	Number of Respondents
2			
3								
4											
5									
6			
7	
8		

Use the dot plot you made to answer each question.

2. If the water park can only choose three raft sizes, how many seats should the three sizes have? Explain your reasoning.

_____

_____

3. If the park can choose five raft sizes, should one of the sizes be an 8-seat raft? Explain your answer.

_____

_____

4. If the park can choose three raft sizes and they plan to order a total of 300 rafts, how many of each size raft should they order? Explain your reasoning.

_____

_____

_____

       Peoples Common Core Mathematics

Make It Work

Answer the questions below.

1. Which type of statistical plot uses a number line and groups of dots to represent data?

   A. line graph
   B. dot plot
   C. histogram
   D. circle graph

2. What is not easy to see on a dot plot?

   A. clusters
   B. gaps
   C. outliers
   D. mean

3. Describe when you would use a dot plot to display statistical data.

   _____

   _____

Use the dot plot to answers Questions 4 and 5.

4. An architect is designing a new high school building full of classrooms. He polls the current teachers to see about how many students are in each one of their classes. The results are shown in the dot plot. If there can be only two sizes of classrooms, how many desks should be in each classroom size? Explain your reasoning.

   Number of Students in Classes

   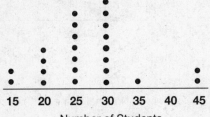

   Number of Students

   _____

   _____

5. Based on the data, the architect decides that there should be three classroom sizes. If all of the existing classes must be moved to the new building before the school year is out, how many classrooms must have 45 desks assuming the same teacher does not teach both of the large classes? Explain your reasoning.

   _____

   _____

   _____

Lesson 45 Displaying Data in Histograms

6.SP.4 Display numerical data in plots on a number line, including dot plots, histograms, and box plots.

6.SP.5.c Giving quantitative measures of center (median and/or mean) and variability (interquartile range and/or mean absolute deviation), as well as describing any overall pattern and any striking deviations from the overall pattern with reference to the context in which the data were gathered.

Real World Connections

Key Words

raw data
bar graph
histogram
frequency table

Janelle recorded the number of hours that a battery lasted in 12 different MP3 players. Here are the results.

12, 9, 10, 15, 11, 14, 18, 10, 21, 16, 22, 14

Display the data in a histogram. How many more batteries lasted from 10 to 14 hours compared with those that lasted from 15 to 19 hours?

When data is collected using statistical questions, the **raw data** is the entire list of all the data collected. The data has not yet been analyzed or summarized. To answer questions about raw data, it is useful to organize and display the data in some sort of graph.

A **bar graph** is a data display that uses horizontal or vertical parallel bars to show numerical amounts for different categories of data. In a bar graph, one bar is used for each category. The length or height of the bar represents the value for that category. Bar graphs are used to make comparisons and trends easier to see. An example of a bar graph is at the right.

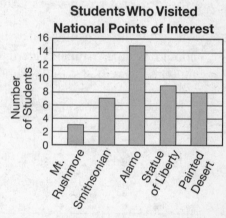

A **histogram** is a special type of bar graph that displays data grouped in equal intervals. It is used to compare the frequency of intervals of the data. You can present the same information in a table, known as a **frequency table**; however, a histogram usually makes it easier to see relationships. Unlike a bar graph, a histogram would not be used for data that is not numerical. An example of a histogram is at the right.

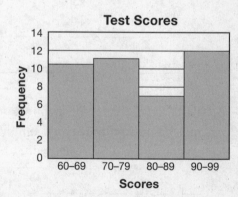

For all types of data displays, it is very important that appropriate titles and labels be included. This ensures that the data makes sense to the person reading the display.

Copying is illegal.
Peoples Common Core Mathematics

Take It Apart

To display data in a histogram, follow some simple steps.

Step 1 Make a frequency table. To do this, examine the raw data and divide it into equal intervals. The lengths of the intervals will depend on the values in the data. Make sure the intervals will include the least and greatest data values.

Raw Data: 12, 9, 10, 15, 11, 14, 18, 10, 21, 16, 22, 14

Step 2 Complete the frequency table. Record the data for each interval, using tally marks. Count the marks to record each frequency.

Hours	Tally	Frequency
5–9	|	1
10–14	⦀⦀ |	6
15–19	|||	3
20–24	||	2

Step 3 Make a histogram. Title the graph and label the axes. Choose a vertical scale. The vertical scale must go at least as high as the highest count in your frequency table. Then draw a bar for each interval.

Step 4 Use the histogram to answer the question.

Compare the heights of the bars. The interval 10–14 has a frequency of 6 and the interval 15–19 has a frequency of 3. The difference is 3, so 3 more batteries lasted from 10 to 14 hours compared with those that lasted from 15 to 19 hours.

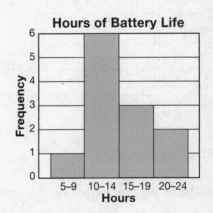

Use the strategy above to complete the histogram for the data shown in the frequency table. Then use the histogram to answer the questions.

Class Size at Bridge Falls Middle School

Intervals	Tally	Frequency
0–9	|	1
10–19	⦀⦀ |	6
20–29	⦀⦀ ⦀⦀ ⦀⦀	15
30–39	⦀⦀ ⦀⦀ ||	12

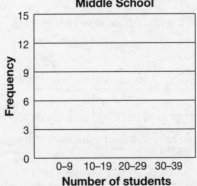

1. How many classes have from 10 to 29 students? _____

2. How many classes have fewer than 20 students? _____

Put It Together

Use what you now know about displaying data to complete a frequency table and a histogram for the situation described below.

To determine the age appeal of a new movie, publicists recorded the ages of the first 25 people who came to a preview showing. The raw data is shown at the right. Make a histogram for the data.

59	21	32	33	40
51	23	23	28	26
35	49	48	41	37
39	44	54	53	29
28	29	57	58	46

Ages	Tally	Frequency
20–29		
30–39		
40–49		
50–59		

Use your histogram above to answer each question.

1. Why were the intervals 0–9 and 10–19 not included on the display?

   _____

2. How many people attending the preview were not in their twenties? Explain how you found your answer.

   _____

3. One person from this group is chosen at random to receive two free movie tickets. In which interval is that person's age most likely to fall? Explain your reasoning.

   _____

   _____

Make It Work

Answer the questions below.

1. Two hundred people are surveyed about their favorite hot dog topping. Which two graphs could show the data and compare the popularity of different toppings chosen?

   A. circle graph and histogram

   B. line graph and bar graph

   C. circle graph and bar graph

   D. histogram and bar graph

2. At camp, 18 students had the following average bowling scores: 92, 70, 91, 105, 100, 95, 85, 98, 85, 107, 92, 83, 99, 118, 88, 79, 110, 64. If you make a histogram using intervals of 10, which interval will have the tallest bar?

   A. 100–109

   B. 90–99

   C. 80–89

   D. 70–79

Use the histogram at the right to answer questions 3 – 5.

3. How many students read 9 books or more? Explain how you found your answer.

_____

4. How many more students read from 9 to 14 books than students who read from 0 to 8 books? Explain how you found your answer.

_____

_____

_____

_____

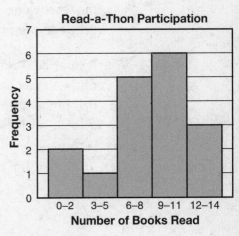

5. Is the statement that follows accurate? Explain your answer. "The histogram shows that 5 students read 7 books."

_____

_____

6.SP.4   Display numerical data in plots on a number line, including dot plots, histograms, and box plots.

6.SP.5.c   Giving quantitative measures of center (median and/or mean) and variability (interquartile range and/or mean absolute deviation), as well as describing any overall pattern and any striking deviations from the overall pattern with reference to the context in which the data were gathered.

Real World Connections

Key Words

box-and-whisker plot

upper extreme

lower extreme

quartile

upper quartile

lower quartile

interquartile range

Roberto kept track of the number of email messages he received at work each day. Make a box-and-whisker plot to represent the data.

Number of Emails Each Day

17	20	22	18	8	19	10	10	17	9
15	21	7	8	20	18	14	22	19	11

A **box-and-whisker plot**, also sometimes called a *box plot*, is a statistical display that summarizes data by showing how data are distributed within a range of values. It consists of a *rectangular box* to represent the middle 50% of a set of data and has *whiskers* (lines) at both ends to represent the other 50% of the data. Box-and-whisker plots are used to display five important values of a data set—the upper extreme, lower extreme, median, upper quartile, and lower quartile.

The **upper extreme** is the greatest value in a data set and the **lower extreme** is the least value in the data set. Recall that the range of a data set is the difference between the greatest value and the least value.

A **quartile** is one of four equal parts of a data set. The **upper quartile** is the median of the upper half of the data set. The **lower quartile** is the median of the lower half of the data set. The **interquartile range** is the difference between the upper quartile and the lower quartile.

An example of a box-and-whisker plot is shown below.

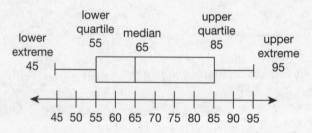

Take It Apart

Follow these steps to display Roberto's data in a box-and-whisker plot.

Step 1 List the number of emails each day in order from least to greatest value.

7 8 8 9 10 10 11 14 15 17 17 18 18 19 19 20 20 21 22 22

The lower extreme is 7. The upper extreme is 22. These extremes are the ends of the *whiskers*.

Step 2 Find the median of the data. There are 20 data values, so the median is the average of the two middle values.

$$\frac{17 + 17}{2} = \frac{34}{2} = 17$$

Step 3 Find the upper and lower quartiles of the data set. There are 10 data values in each half of the data, so find the average of the two middle numbers in each half of the data.

The upper quartile is $\frac{19 + 20}{2} = \frac{39}{2} = 19.5$. The lower quartile is $\frac{10 + 10}{2} = \frac{20}{2} = 10$.

These values are the ends of the box.

Step 4 Draw the box-and-whisker plot. Create a number line to show the range of the data in equal intervals. Plot points for the lower and upper extremes, the upper and lower quartiles, and the median. Draw a box with ends at the quartiles. Draw a line within the box to indicate the median. To make the whiskers, connect the lower and upper extremes to the box with lines. Be sure to title the plot.

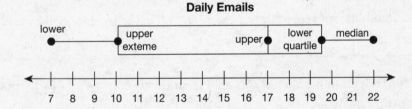

Find the five values that are needed to create a box-and-whisker plot for each set of data.

1. 95, 78, 67, 84, 72, 88, 92

2. 46, 52, 38, 44, 51, 39, 50, 42

_____

_____

_____

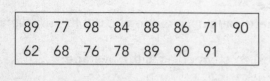 **Put It Together**

Draw a box-and-whisker plot for each set of data.

1. the exam grades of 15 students

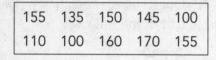

Math Test Grades

2. the number of customers who visited a store for 10 consecutive days

Visitors to Store

Use the box-and-whisker plot to answer each question.

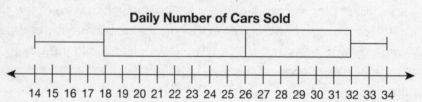

3. What is the median number of cars sold?

_____

4. What is the range of the number of cars sold?

_____

5. Is it possible to find the mean number of cars sold from the display? Why or why not?

_____

_____

_____

6. Is it possible to find the mode number of cars sold from the display? Why or why not?

_____

_____

_____

Make It Work

Answer the questions below.

1. Which measure of central tendency can be determined from a box-and-whisker plot?

A. mean

B. median

C. mode

D. All of these.

2. What is the interquartile range of this box-and-whisker plot?

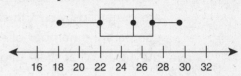

A. 27   **B.** 12

C. 5   **D.** 3

Use the box-and-whisker plot to answer each question.

3. Louisa recorded the number of cricket chirps from 7:00 P.M. to 7:01 P.M. for 20 days. According to the box-and-whisker plot, what was the maximum number of cricket chirps during the 20-day period? Explain how you determined your answer.

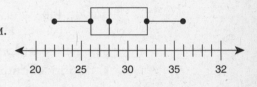

_____

_____

4. Is it possible to determine the number of days in the 20-day period that the number of cricket chirps was at most 26 chirps? If so, state the number of days and explain how you found your answer.

_____

_____

_____

5. On how many days did the number of cricket chirps range between 26 and 32 chirps? Explain your reasoning.

_____

_____

Lesson 47 Reporting and Describing Observations

6.SP.5.a Reporting the number of observations.
6.SP.5.b Describing the nature of the attribute under investigation, including how it was measured and its units of measurement.

Real World Connections

Key Words

observation

categorical data

numerical data

A skateboard company makes 1,000 skateboards each month. It makes 5 different models. The number of each model manufactured depends on which models are preferred by customers. If the company wants to make a statistical display to compare the number of each model it manufactures, which type of graph should they use? What scale might they use on the graph?

When choosing the best statistical display for a set of data, it is helpful to consider the number of observations and the nature of the attribute under investigation (what is being studied).

When gathering information using statistical questions, an **observation** is a response to the question. The total number of observations is the same as the total number of responses. For example, if 50 sixth grade students complete a survey, the number of observations for each question on the survey should be 50.

The nature of some data is categorical while the nature of other data is numerical. **Categorical data** consists of data that can be sorted into categories. Here are some examples: favorite fruit, favorite color car, kind of snack you like, brand of tennis shoe you prefer, and so on. Bar graphs are particularly useful for reporting this type of data.

Numerical data consists of observations that must have a number value. Here are some examples: number of books you read, hours per week spent watching TV, number of pets you own, how much your backpack weighs, and so on. Dot plots, histograms, and box-and-whisker plots are particularly useful when describing this type of data.

Here is a list that describes what the different statistical displays best report.

- *Bar graph*: compares data that can be sorted into categories
- *Dot plot*: compares the frequencies of small sets of numerical data
- *Histogram*: compares the frequencies of intervals of numerical data
- *Line graph*: shows changes in data over time
- *Circle graph*: shows how parts of a whole compare to the whole

 Peoples Common Core Mathematics

Take It Apart

To best report the skateboard company's data, follow some simple steps.

Step 1   Read the problem on the previous page carefully. Decide whether the attribute being investigated is categorical or numerical.

        Since the 5 models can be sorted into categories (for example Model A, Model B, and so on), the attribute under investigation is categorical.

Step 2   Choose an appropriate graph.

        A bar graph is the most effective for comparing categorical data.

Step 3   Choose a scale for the graph.

        The total number of observations being reported is 1,000. However, there are 5 categories. If they were divided evenly, the number of observations in each category would be 200, but you do not yet know if they are divided evenly. To be safe, you should choose a scale that is somewhat bigger than 200, such as 400 in increments of 25 or 50.

Determine whether the nature of each of the following attributes is *categorical* or *numerical*.

1. per hour pay rate

      _____

2. eye color

      _____

3. brand of toothpaste you use

      _____

4. number of minutes you exercise each week

      _____

Determine which type of statistical display would be most effective for each situation.

5. Find how many more teenagers spend from $200 to $299 of their own money on school clothes each year as compared to those who spend from $100 to $199.

      _____

6. Show the fraction of a monthly budget spent on groceries.

      _____

Put It Together

Use what you now know about different types of data to determine whether the nature of each of the following attributes is *categorical* or *numerical*.

1. number of hours you study each day
   _____

2. how many miles you must drive to reach the closest movie theater
   _____

3. the name of the closest big city to your home
   _____

4. the vegetable you eat most often
   _____

Answer each question.

5. Explain why clothes sizes can be either categorical or numerical data. Give an example of each.

   _____

   _____

   _____

6. The local paper wants to show the public that its circulation has been consistently growing over the past five years. Which statistical display would be most effective in this situation? Why?

   _____

   _____

   _____

7. Explain why the total number of observations for a set of data is not shown on a circle graph. Give an example to support your answer.

   _____

   _____

   _____

           Peoples Common Core Mathematics

 ## Make It Work

Answer the questions below.

1. Which set of data could best be represented in a bar graph?

   A. the population of a city each year for the past 8 years

   B. the number of text messages sent by teenagers per week

   C. the number of days of snow in four cities last winter

   D. the growth of a seed over the course of a week

2. Which graph would be least appropriate to report the results of the election for class president?

   A. a bar graph

   B. a circle graph

   C. a line graph

   D. a dot plot

3. Explain why school grades could be either categorical data or numerical data. Give an example of each.

   _____

   _____

   _____

4. A cell phone company conducted an online survey in which they asked 2,000 customers to indicate whether the weight, appearance, signal strength, or accessories of a cell phone were most important to them. The results are shown in the table at the right. The company plans to report the data in a bar graph. Based on the total number of observations and the number of observations in each category, choose a highest value for the vertical axis and an appropriate scale for the graph. Explain how you arrived at your answer.

Customer Preferences	
Weight	600
Appearance	375
Signal	800
Accessories	225

   _____

   _____

5. Explain how to determine the total number of observations from a bar graph whose vertical axis is labeled "Frequency (in thousands)".

   _____

   _____

Lesson 48 Relating Data to the Context in Which It Was Gathered

6.SP.5.d Relating the choice of measures of center and variability to the shape of the data distribution and the context in which the data were gathered.

Real World Connections

Key Word

variability

The manager of an arcade wants information about the ages of the arcade's customers. One day, he records the ages of the first 20 customers.

12	15	11	14	43	13	14	14	58	14
15	11	16	13	52	17	12	14	15	10

Which measure(s) of central tendency will give the manager the best information about the age of most of his customers?

Recall that there are three measures of central tendency: mean, median, and mode. Each one describes the "middle" of the data, but in a different way. The *mean* describes the average of all the data values; the *median* is the halfway point of the data, with 50% of the data below it and 50% above it; and the *mode* represents the outcome that happened more frequently than any other data.

Any one of these measures could be used to describe the central tendency of the data, but in most cases, the data itself determines which is most accurate. For example, **mean** is very sensitive to outliers when the data set is small, while the other two measures are not. In such a case, the mean of the data is not very accurate.

Occasionally, you will want to use a different kind of descriptive statistic, called variability, to describe a data set. **Variability** is a measure of how spread out, or dispersed, a set of data is. The simplest measure of variability is range. Consider a store that sells television sets. If they want to reach the biggest group of customers possible, they might advertise that they have a wide **range** of prices, from inexpensive all the way to very expensive.

Take It Apart

Follow these steps to determine which measure(s) of central tendency will give the arcade manager the best information.

Step 1 Find the mean of the data.

$$\frac{\text{sum of the data values}}{\text{number of data values}} = \frac{383}{20} = 19.15$$

12	15	11	14	43	13	14	14	58	14
15	11	16	13	52	17	12	14	15	10

Step 2 Find the median of the data.

10, 11, 11, 12, 12, 13, 13, 14, 14, ⑭ ⑭, 14, 15, 15, 15, 16, 17, 43, 52, 58

The middle two numbers are 14 and 14 so the median is $\frac{14 + 14}{2} = \frac{28}{2} = 14$.

Step 3 Find the mode of the data.

The mode is 14 since it appears the most often.

Step 4 Compare each of the measures to the raw data and see which one best represents it.

A quick glance at the data indicates that most of the customers were young teenagers. In fact, 17 of the 20 were teenagers, so the mode (14) and median (14) both provide good descriptions of the data. However, since only 3 of the customers were above the mean (19.15), and they were considerably above the mean, the mean does not provide a good description of the data.

Use the strategy above to determine which measure of central tendency better describes the data. Circle the correct answer.

1. 25, 29, 19, 19, 28, 27, 30

   median   mode

2. 100, 88, 100, 92, 87, 76, 35

   median   mode

3. 20, 20, 20, 25, 75, 22

   mean   mode

4. 44, 51, 76, 22, 22, 58, 63

   mean   mode

Lesson 48 **Relating Data to the Context in Which It Was Gathered**

Put It Together

Use what you now know about measures of central tendency to answer each question.

1. Fifty customers were surveyed about their favorite color of tennis shoe. Which measure of central tendency would best predict which color shoe would sell out the fastest?

_____

2. Woo found the following prices for polo shirts: $22, $27, $25, $21, $40, $29, and $25. Which measure of central tendency is most affected by the $40 shirt?

_____

Answer each question.

3. The table at the right shows the hourly wages of eight employees at a bike shop. Explain why the median best describes the wages.

Employees' Hourly Wages	
$5.70	$7.00
$5.70	$7.25
$5.70	$7.50
$6.50	$16.00

_____

_____

_____

4. Create a set of 5 different data values for which the mean and the median are equally good representations of the data.

_____

_____

5. The producers of a new movie brag that it is going to attract viewers of all ages. To support this claim, the producers recorded the ages of the first 100 people who came to the movie on opening day. Which statistical measure is the only one that should be high if the producers are correct? Explain your reasoning.

_____

_____

_____

_____

Make It Work

Answer the questions below.

1. Which measure of central tendency is most affected by an outlier in the data set?

   A. mean

   B. median

   C. mode

   D. They are all affected equally.

2. The weekly earnings of four workers are $620, $600, $980, and $610. Which measure of central tendency best describes what a fifth worker doing the same job might expect to earn weekly?

   A. mean

   B. median

   C. mode

   D. range

3. Lisa recorded her weekly earnings below. Does the mean or the mode best describe Lisa's typical weekly earnings? Why?

   $50, $50, $50, $45, $50, $50, $180

   _____

   _____

   _____

4. Which measure of central tendency must be used to describe data that is not numerical, such as favorite color? Why?

   _____

   _____

   _____

5. Samantha is recording the daily high temperatures for the month of July in Florida. Before she even begins recording the data, she predicts that the mean will be an excellent measure of central tendency to describe the data. Explain why Samantha is most likely correct.

   _____

   _____

   _____

Kick It Up!

Question 1: How do you write the right questions?

Survey questions can be tricky to write. They must be designed in such a way that the information is useful and unbiased. Unbiased means that the wording of the question does not favor any particular answer.

Pretend your school has its own movie theater and shows a movie every Friday afternoon. Cool, right? Now pretend you are in charge of selecting the movie (PG only) for next week. Design a survey to help you select the movie that will please the most people. Don't be too specific – try to get as much useful information as you can with just 2 or 3 questions.

Compare your questions with a classmate. Discuss whether any of your questions are biased and if so, try to reword them so they are not.

Question 2: How tall did you say?

Everybody knows that professional basketball players are tall. But do you know the average height of a professional basketball player? Would you like to?

Use the internet to research any professional basketball team. Record the names and heights of all the players in a table after converting the heights to inches. Calculate the mean, median, and mode of the data and then convert them back to feet and inches. Record these values under your table.

Which measure represents the average height for the players on your team?

Compare your results to those of classmates who chose different teams than you did. Which team has the tallest average height? That's really tall!

Question 3: How many text messages are floating around cyberspace?

Text messaging is all the rage. There must be millions of text messages sent and received every day, maybe even every hour. That's a lot of messages floating around!

Survey 30 older students at your school or in your neighborhood. Ask each person approximately how many text messages they send per day. Record the results.

 Peoples Common Core Mathematics

Use your data to create a histogram. First, decide on an appropriate scale for the vertical axis and interval lengths for the horizontal axis. Then create a frequency table. Use the frequencies to draw the histogram. Don't forget to give your display a title.

Compare your findings with your classmates.

Then consider this—would your results have been significantly different if you had surveyed 30 parents, rather than students? Why?

Now try it and see!

Question 4: Can a professional athlete be a grandparent?

Are there any professional athletes that are old enough to be a grandparent? Sure, there are just a few and they most likely play golf or baseball. For example, in 2010, Jamie Moyer of the Philadelphia Phillies was 47 years old and although he wasn't a grandfather then, he certainly could have been.

Baseball is probably the team sport with the greatest age range for its players. Use the internet to research any major league baseball team. Make a list of the ages of all the players. From this list, create a box-and-whisker plot to display the data.

What is the median age for your team? What is the range of ages for your team? Are any of the players on your team old enough to be a grandfather?

Compare your findings with your classmates.

Rubric for Evaluating Math Assignments

Points	Criteria
4	A 4-point response shows a thorough understanding of the essential mathematical concepts of the problem. The student executes procedures correctly and gives relevant responses to all parts of the task. The response contains a clear, effective explanation detailing how the problem was solved and why decisions were made. The response contains few minor errors, if any.
3	A 3-point response shows a nearly complete understanding of the problem's essential mathematical concepts. The student executes nearly all procedures and gives relevant responses to most parts of the task. The response may contain a correct numerical answer, but the required work is not provided or the response may contain minor errors.
2	A 2-point response shows limited understanding of the essential mathematical concepts of the problem. The response and procedures may be incomplete and/or may contain major errors. The explanation of how the problem was solved and why decisions were made may be confusing.
1	A 1-point response shows insufficient understanding of the problem's essential mathematical concepts. The procedures, if any, contain major errors. There may be no explanation of the solution or the reader is unable to understand how and why decisions were made.
0	A 0-point response is irrelevant, illegible, incomprehensible, or shows that no legitimate attempt was made to solve the problem.

TABLE 1. Common addition and subtraction situations.[6]

	Result Unknown	Change Unknown	Start Unknown
Add to	Two bunnies sat on the grass. Three more bunnies hopped there. How many bunnies are on the grass now? $2 + 3 = ?$	Two bunnies were sitting on the grass. Some more bunnies hopped there. Then there were five bunnies. How many bunnies hopped over to the first two? $2 + ? = 5$	Some bunnies were sitting on the grass. Three more bunnies hopped there. Then there were five bunnies. How many bunnies were on the grass before? $? + 3 = 5$
Take from	Five apples were on the table. I ate two apples. How many apples are on the table now? $5 - 2 = ?$	Five apples were on the table. I ate some apples. Then there were three apples. How many apples did I eat? $5 - ? = 3$	Some apples were on the table. I ate two apples. Then there were three apples. How many apples were on the table before? $? - 2 = 3$

	Total Unknown	Addend Unknown	Both Addends Unknown[1]
Put Together/ Take Apart[2]	Three red apples and two green apples are on the table. How many apples are on the table? $3 + 2 = ?$	Five apples are on the table. Three are red and the rest are green. How many apples are green? $3 + ? = 5,\ 5 - 3 = ?$	Grandma has five flowers. How many can she put in her red vase and how many in her blue vase? $5 = 0 + 5, 5 = 5 + 0$ $5 = 1 + 4, 5 = 4 + 1$ $5 = 2 + 3, 5 = 3 + 2$

	Difference Unknown	Bigger Unknown	Smaller Unknown
Compare[3]	("How many more?" version): Lucy has two apples. Julie has five apples. How many more apples does Julie have than Lucy? ("How many fewer?" version): Lucy has two apples. Julie has five apples. How many fewer apples does Lucy have than Julie? $2 + ? = 5,\ 5 - 2 = ?$	(Version with "more"): Julie has three more apples than Lucy. Lucy has two apples. How many apples does Julie have? (Version with "fewer"): Lucy has 3 fewer apples than Julie. Lucy has two apples. How many apples does Julie have? $2 + 3 = ?,\ 3 + 2 = ?$	(Version with "more"): Julie has three more apples than Lucy. Julie has five apples. How many apples does Lucy have? (Version with "fewer"): Lucy has 3 fewer apples than Julie. Julie has five apples. How many apples does Lucy have? $5 - 3 = ?,\ ? + 3 = 5$

[1]These take apart situations can be used to show all the decompositions of a given number. The associated equations, which have the total on the left of the equal sign, help children understand that the = sign does not always mean makes or results in but always does mean is the same number as.

[2]Either addend can be unknown, so there are three variations of these problem situations. Both Addends Unknown is a productive extension of this basic situation, especially for small numbers less than or equal to 10.

[3]For the Bigger Unknown or Smaller Unknown situations, one version directs the correct operation (the version using more for the bigger unknown and using less for the smaller unknown). The other versions are more difficult.

[6]Adapted from Box 2-4 of Mathematics Learning in Early Childhood, National Research Council (2009, pp. 32, 33).

TABLE 2. Common multiplication and division situations.[7]

	Unknown Product	Group Size Unknown ("How many in each group?" Division)	Number of Groups Unknown ("How many groups?" Division)
	$3 \times 6 = ?$	$3 \times ? = 18$, and $18 \div 3 = ?$	$? \times 6 = 18$, and $18 \div 6 = ?$
Equal Groups	There are 3 bags with 6 plums in each bag. How many plums are there in all? *Measurement example.* You need 3 lengths of string, each 6 inches long. How much string will you need altogether?	If 18 plums are shared equally into 3 bags, then how many plums will be in each bag? *Measurement example.* You have 18 inches of string, which you will cut into 3 equal pieces. How long will each piece of string be?	If 18 plums are to be packed 6 to a bag, then how many bags are needed? *Measurement example.* You have 18 inches of string, which you will cut into pieces that are 6 inches long. How many pieces of string will you have?
Arrays,[4] Area[5]	There are 3 rows of apples with 6 apples in each row. How many apples are there? *Area example.* What is the area of a 3 cm by 6 cm rectangle?	If 18 apples are arranged into 3 equal rows, how many apples will be in each row? *Area example.* A rectangle has area 18 square centimeters. If one side is 3 cm long, how long is a side next to it?	If 18 apples are arranged into equal rows of 6 apples, how many rows will there be? *Area example.* A rectangle has area 18 square centimeters. If one side is 6 cm long, how long is a side next to it?
Compare	A blue hat costs $6. A red hat costs 3 times as much as the blue hat. How much does the red hat cost? *Measurement example.* A rubber band is 6 cm long. How long will the rubber band be when it is stretched to be 3 times as long?	A red hat costs $18 and that is 3 times as much as a blue hat costs. How much does a blue hat cost? *Measurement example.* A rubber band is stretched to be 18 cm long and that is 3 times as long as it was at first. How long was the rubber band at first?	A red hat costs $18 and a blue hat costs $6. How many times as much does the red hat cost as the blue hat? *Measurement example.* A rubber band was 6 cm long at first. Now it is stretched to be 18 cm long. How many times as long is the rubber band now as it was at first?
General	$a \times b = ?$	$a \times ? = p$, and $p \div a = ?$	$? \times b = p$, and $p \div b = ?$

[4]The language in the array examples shows the easiest form of array problems. A harder form is to use the terms rows and columns: The apples in the grocery window are in 3 rows and 6 columns. How many apples are in there? Both forms are valuable.

[5]Area involves arrays of squares that have been pushed together so that there are no gaps or overlaps, so array problems include these especially important measurement situations.

---

[7]The first examples in each cell are examples of discrete things. These are easier for students and should be given before the measurement examples.

TABLE 3. The properties of operations. Here a, b and c stand for arbitrary numbers in a given number system. The properties of operations apply to the rational number system, the real number system, and the complex number system.

Associative property of addition	$(a + b) + c = a + (b + c)$
Commutative property of addition	$a + b = b + a$
Additive identity property of 0	$a + 0 = 0 + a = a$
Existence of additive inverses	For every a there exists $-a$ so that $a + (-a) = (-a) + a = 0$.
Associative property of multiplication	$(a \times b) \times c = a \times (b \times c)$
Commutative property of multiplication	$a \times b = b \times a$
Multiplicative identity property of 1	$a \times 1 = 1 \times a = a$
Existence of multiplicative inverses	For every $a \neq 0$ there exists $1/a$ so that $a \times 1/a = 1/a \times a = 1$.
Distributive property of multiplication over addition	$a \times (b + c) = a \times b + a \times c$

TABLE 4. The properties of equality. Here a, b and c stand for arbitrary numbers in the rational, real, or complex number systems.

Reflexive property of equality	$a = a$
Symmetric property of equality	If $a = b$, then $b = a$.
Transitive property of equality	If $a = b$ and $b = c$, then $a = c$.
Addition property of equality	If $a = b$, then $a + c = b + c$.
Subtraction property of equality	If $a = b$, then $a - c = b - c$.
Multiplication property of equality	If $a = b$, then $a \times c = b \times c$.
Division property of equality	If $a = b$ and $c \neq 0$, then $a \div c = b \div c$.
Substitution property of equality	If $a = b$, then b may be substituted for a in any expression containing a.

TABLE 5. The properties of inequality. Here a, b and c stand for arbitrary numbers in the rational or real number systems.

Exactly one of the following is true: $a < b$, $a = b$, $a > b$.
If $a > b$ and $b > c$ then $a > c$.
If $a > b$, then $b < a$.
If $a > b$, then $-a < -b$.
If $a > b$, then $a \pm c > b \pm c$.
If $a > b$ and $c > 0$, then $a \times c > b \times c$.
If $a > b$ and $c < 0$, then $a \times c < b \times c$.
If $a > b$ and $c > 0$, then $a \div c > b \div c$.
If $a > b$ and $c < 0$, then $a \div c < b \div c$.

Notes

Copying is permitted.